# The ULTIMATE book of MONEY HINTS

Hundreds of tips on how to save money at home, in the office and on holiday

**BayBooks**
An imprint of HarperCollins*Publishers*

**A Bay Books Publication**
An imprint of HarperCollins *Publishers*

First published in Australia in 1995

Copyright © Bay Books, 1995

This book is copyright.
Apart from any fair dealing for the purposes of private study, research, criticism or review, as permitted under the Copyright Act, no part may be reproduced by any process without written permission.
Inquiries should be addressed to the publishers.

**Bay Books**
25 Ryde Road, Pymble, Sydney NSW 2073, Australia
31 Glenview Road, Auckland 10, New Zealand

National Library of Australia Cataloguing-in-Publication data:
Swanton, Liz.
  The ultimate book of money hints.

  ISBN 1 86378 245 1
  1. Home economics–Handbooks, manuals, etc. 2. Finance, Personal–Handbooks, manuals, etc. I. Title. (Series: Ultimate hints series).
  Includes index.

640.42

Cover and internal illustrations by Sue Ninham
Printed in Australia by Griffin Paperbacks

9 8 7 6 5 4 3 2 1
97 96 95 94

# CONTENTS

INTRODUCTION ■ 5

A WORD OF WARNING... ■ 7

CLEAN UP THE SAVINGS ■ 9

WINE, DINE, HAVE FUN AND TRAVEL ■ 11

HEATING, COOLING AND LIGHTING ■ 17

SAVING MONEY WITH YOUR CAR ■ 25

FINANCIAL FASHION ■ 31

FOOD AND COOKING ■ 35

GOOD VALUE GARDENING ■ 45

GENERAL MONEY-SAVING TIPS ■ 53

GREAT GIFT GIVING ■ 57

HEALTH, HYGIENE AND BEAUTY ■ 61

BORROWING AND BUDGETING ■ 69

OFFICE SAVINGS ■ 73

PENNYWISE PEST CONTROL ■ 77

RECYCLING ■ 85

RENOVATING ■ 89

CENT-SIBLE SHOPPING ■ 95

MULTIPURPOSE MONEY SAVERS ■ 99

DOING THE LAUNDRY ■ 109

INDEX ■ 112

# INTRODUCTION

Unless we're on the list of Australia's 200 wealthiest people, we're all interested in saving money — and probably part of the reason they are on that list is because at one stage they were too.

No matter what the income, most of us need to find ways to stretch it that little bit further, and that's what this book is all about.

Even if you only adopt a couple of the suggestions, you'll still end up with an extra dollar or two in your pocket: money that could be saved, or spent on other more interesting things.

The best way to save, though, is by getting the whole family involved. Why not discuss some of the ideas we've listed? You might be saving for something special or forced to cut back on outgoings because of financial difficulties. Talk to everyone in the family about what you're trying to do and why. Then everyone can work out how they can contribute.

It's a great way to teach your children how to be financially wise, and everyone benefits in the long run from being involved as a team. We save money for the present and the future, and our children learn a lesson that they'll be able to pass on to their children.

Waste is not smart. These days so much of our waste is affecting our environment too. Many of the ideas in this book pay dividends not only in terms of our bank accounts and wallets, but also for the improved health of ourselves and our earth. Perhaps those are the greatest savings of all.

# A WORD OF WARNING...

In certain sections of this book, instructions have been given for making your own cleaning liquids, or using alternatives to commercial preparations.

In many cases the alternative is more 'natural' but that doesn't necessarily mean it is harmless. Care should always be taken with any form of cleaning agent because too much of anything can be harmful.

Exercise care when making your own cleansers or using alternative solutions, and make sure they are carefully packed, well labelled and stored out of reach of children, preferably in a locked cupboard that doesn't have the key left in the door. Make sure these mixtures are never stored in empty food or drink containers that might be both attractive and confusing to a child — or to an adult who can't read or understand the label you've written.

When using anything highly concentrated or that could be harmful, wear rubber gloves and work in a well-ventilated area. Make sure children and pets cannot make contact with the product.

If something is spilled or swallowed and you're not sure of the possible outcome, contact your nearest doctor or Poisons Information Centre immediately. Make sure you can tell them exactly what's involved and approximately how much. In fact, as soon as you have read this, go and write down the telephone numbers of your local doctor, chemist, hospital and poisons centre and stick the piece of paper close to the phone. Also talk to your doctor or chemist about keeping a poisons kit at home.

(If you are considering making your own cleaning compounds or using alternatives, it might be a good idea to put on the label exactly what the ingredients are so you have a ready reference if the worst happens and it becomes necessary to know immediately.)

If you're using any type of machine or power tool, please follow the safety instructions, and make sure you cultivate the habit of wearing gloves and safety goggles whenever you're doing work around the house that may make dust, particles or larger objects fly off from walls, floors or ceilings.

Remember, too, that ultimately it is 'buyer beware'. This is a book about saving money, but it's up to you to accept that you only get what you pay for and to make sure your money works for you.

# CLEAN UP THE SAVINGS

- Forget investing in expensive window-cleaning preparations. Fill a pump-spray container with a mix of half ammonia and half water. It also works well on taps and other sink fittings. For another alternative, put 120 mL ammonia, 25 mL of vinegar and 1 L of warm water into a spray bottle and spray on glass, mirrors or fittings. Wipe down with a clean cloth or crumpled newspaper.

- An all-purpose household cleaner: 4 L of hot water, with 50 mL each of cloudy ammonia and vinegar, and 1 tablespoon of bicarbonate of soda. Mix well and pour into pump-spray bottles. Use when necessary with a cloth.

- A good cleaning agent for uncoated copper is Worcestershire sauce. Rub on with a soft cloth and then polish with another dry cloth. Or mix salt and lemon juice to a paste. Rub on with one cloth, polish off with another. Or simply dip half a lemon in salt and rub it over the surface. Then rinse, dry, and polish with a soft cloth.

- A simple, cheap and effective furniture polish: strain ½ cup of lemon juice and mix with 1 cup of olive oil in a bottle. Shake well before dampening a soft rag with the mixture and applying to furniture. Polish off with another soft rag.

- Slate, lino and tiles will sparkle if they're wiped over with ½ cup of vinegar mixed into a bucket of warm water.

- Make your own oven cleaner by combining 4 L of hot water, 100 mL each cloudy ammonia and vinegar, and 2 tablespoons of bicarbonate of soda. The solution is safe but it is still advisable to wear gloves when scrubbing.

- An easier way to clean your oven (and, like the first option, more environmentally friendly and cheaper than commercial oven cleaners) is to place 50 mL of ammonia in a shallow glass dish and add enough water to cover the bottom of the container. Heat the oven for 20 minutes, then turn off and put the ammonia-water mix inside and leave overnight. Baked-on food will be loosened and you can finish the cleaning job with some bicarbonate of soda and warm water on a sponge. Rinse clean. This is also a lot kinder to your hands and your eyes than a normal commercial preparation.

- Polishing silver is cheap and easy. Save your aluminium foil, put a small lump of it in a salt and water solution and add the silver object which needs cleaning. Leave for a minute or two, then dry and rub with a soft cloth.

• Washing dishes? Whether you're handwashing or using a machine, rinse dirty dishes in cold water and stack until you have a full load. Before rinsing pans and dishes that may have oil or fat residue on them, wipe it off with some newspaper and add the paper to the compost heap.

• Washing and peeling vegetables? Do them in a basin of cold water and add the water to the garden or the compost bin.

• There are easier and cheaper ways to eliminate household odours than using expensive deodorant sprays. Try putting a saucer of bicarbonate of soda or vanilla in the fridge, a saucer of vanilla in the toilet or kitchen and a cup of vinegar near the stove. Rub salt or bicarbonate of soda into cutting boards, or rinse them with a bit of vanilla in the water. For day-long freshness, invest a few dollars in an essential-oil burner and warm several drops of oil to freshen the air and lift your mood. You can also be sure you're not allowing any unnatural substance into the air, with the associated damage it might do to you or the environment.

• See the chapter Multipurpose money savers. Many of these things are already in your pantry or would be a welcome addition. A few simple products will tackle a multitude of tasks and complete them with less damage to you and the environment. Because so few do so much they take up much less space than specific products for each specific job. And they're all a great deal cheaper than any one specific product. (See also *The Ultimate Book of Household Hints* published by Bay Books.)

# WINE, DINE, HAVE FUN AND TRAVEL

## WINING AND DINING

### DINING IN

* Eating out at restaurants costs money, even at the so-called cheap eats. Entertaining at home costs too if you as the host pay for everything. Why not try a pot-luck dinner? Invite your friends and ask everyone to bring something to contribute, in addition to whatever they're drinking. As the host you may choose to provide the main course, but ask one friend to take care of the rice, the salad or the vegetables, another to provide dessert, another to bring the bread and perhaps a little something to have with coffee. This way you get to have a great time with friends and no one has broken the bank to do it.

* Using the pot-luck principle, entertain by rotation. Connect regularly with a certain group of friends, taking it in turn to play host. If there are children involved, you can exclude them and organise a sitter or, better still, take them along to be part of the proceedings, making sure you get an early start to allow for a reasonable bedtime. Everyone helps with the preparation, and the clean-up too, so no one spends a day or two in the kitchen either side of the party.

### BABYSITTING

* Babysitting needn't cost a fortune. Set up a club with friends and neighbours to give each other time. Or if you're dining out with friends and both families have children, share the cost of one sitter — the children will enjoy the novelty of bedding down with house guests too!

* Other sources of reasonably priced sitters could be the local nanny or teachers college, or a university, where students need to raise a few extra dollars, or perhaps an elderly neighbour who also needs a few dollars and who would enjoy some time with young children.

### DINING OUT

• If you do choose to dine out, either for work, a social occasion or simply your own sanity, check the specials that are on offer. The dining-out business is fiercely competitive. For example, your local restaurant might offer cut-price meals one night a week, or a two-for-one offer.

• Try somewhere where you can easily share several courses, rather than ordering individual entrees and main courses.

• Consider 'doing' a meal other than dinner; some restaurants and major hotels offer great deals on breakfast or brunch. It could open up a world of new experiences for you, as well as being easier on the budget.

### THE GREAT OUTDOORS

• Picnics are another great way of getting together with friends without the costs and the constraints of a restaurant. Pack a picnic basket yourself, or check with the local delicatessen or specialty food store: they might put together a selection for you. I love night picnics in warm weather — gather some friends, the picnic basket and some chilled champagne or wine and head for the beach or a hill overlooking the city lights. Don't forget the insect spray! Alternatively, just pick up some fish and chips, or a chicken-shop bird and salads. For once, go against your environmental responsibility and take paper plates and serviettes, plastic cutlery and 'glasses' for a total rest away from the dishes. Oh, don't forget the corkscrew, either!

* Lost touch with the neighbours? Why not organise a street party and get everyone to contribute something towards the food and drink. Talk to your local council. If you live in a small street, it may be feasible to close off the street, which will make the event a much safer prospect for the children. Otherwise congregate in the biggest backyard and re-establish that neighbourly feeling for next to nothing.

## ENTERTAINMENT

### FREE FOR FITNESS

* Thinking about buying a boat for some family fun? Why not consider something that is sail- or oar-powered? Motor boats use a lot of fuel, which is expensive and pollutes to the water. Wind is free; oars require arms — and give them exercise.

### FILM AND THEATRE

* All of us have a weakness for a great film or a good piece of theatre but sometimes the cost can be way beyond what the budget dictates that week. Find out about half-price deals at your local cinema. Generally, one night a week is reserved for cheaper seat prices.

* The same goes for theatre. Midweek can be cheaper than weekends and matinees cheaper than an evening show.

* Check your paper for previews, dress rehearsals or charity nights where you'll probably get a little something extra apart from the show — and know that a proportion of the ticket cost is going to a good cause.

### LEARN AND SAVE

* Join a library rather than constantly buying books, or find a book exchange nearby where you can swap your old reads for 'new' ones. Or organise a group with friends, circulating books and magazines among yourselves. If you become really organised, you could arrange among yourselves that each of you takes a subscription to a different magazine and then you hand them around the group.

* Libraries are often good sources of other entertainment; they may offer good films or guest lectures at reasonable prices. And the local video library offers you a wide range of films for a fraction of the price of going to the cinema, with the bonus that you can supply your own snacks for much less than their cost at the theatre.

* Is there a university or tertiary college in your area? You can often find special films, guest lectures, student productions, or even a full night-study course on an interesting topic, at reasonable prices.

* Museums offer similar excitements, apart from the usual collections. Get into the habit of regularly checking the amusement section of your paper for details of all this type of entertainment. There are often plenty of special or free deals going if you're sharp-sighted enough to pick up on them.

### PARTIES

* Save on the cost of ice for chilling drinks when entertaining. The week before the party, fill cake pans with water and freeze. Once there is a solid block of ice, remove it from the pan and wrap in foil. Keep frozen until needed for the drinks container. The blocks will keep cold and solid for hours if kept in the foil. Alternatively, wash out your milk

cartons, fill them three-quarters full with water and freeze.

* Children's party due? Use some edible food colouring to dye water and make a freezer full of different-coloured ice cubes for serving with lemonade or cordial. Pile an assortment of colours into glasses. The kids will love it and it's fun which costs very little. Food colouring is very cheap and can be used to add interest to all areas of the party — the cordial, the cake, the cake's icing, the marshmallows. Or check out your local school-supply shop for a larger quantity of concentrated vegetable colouring such as Edicol, but bear in mind that it is far more concentrated than supermarket-supplied food colouring. I had green fingers for several days after rubbing some through the coconut which was to top my godson's cricket-pitch birthday cake!

* One of the hardest things about entertaining is working out quantities. It's very easy to have not enough (and disappointed guests) or too much (and wasted food and drink). In the table are some suggestions to get it right and keep yourself, your wallet and the visitors happy.

- Wine: 1 bottle provides six average glasses. Calculate on the basis of about one bottle of each type per every four people.
- Fortified spirits: Fortified spirits, such as sherry, vermouth or port provide 12–15 glasses per bottle.
- Spirits: 1 bottle makes about 30 cocktails or 20 mixed or neat drinks.
- Liqueur: 1 bottle offers around 30 drinks.
- Cordial: 1 small bottle equals around 20 drinks.
- Tea and coffee: Calculate on the basis of a quarter to a half more cups than guests, as some people will have a second cup. For 20 cups of tea this means around 70 g of leaf tea or 20 tea bags, 4 L of water, 300 mL of milk and 500 g of sugar; for 20 cups of coffee, this means around 200 g of ground coffee (or 70 g instant), 4 L of water, 500 mL of milk and 500 g of sugar.
- Bread: You will need two large sandwich loaves for 20 sandwiches and 250–300 g of butter or margarine.
- Bread rolls: Work on the basis of one per person plus about one-third again for the people wanting seconds. You'll need 250–300 g of butter or margarine for 20 rolls.
- Meat for sandwiches: Allow 500 g of thinly sliced meat for 10–15 sandwiches.
- Cheese for nibbles: Around 100 g per person or 2 kg (and 1 kg of biscuits) for 20 people; as an end-of-meal treat, about half that amount. However, the more types you have, the more people are likely to eat because they will want to try several, so if you're offering a wide selection, add another 25 per cent to the calculation.
- Soup: Allow 200–250 mL per person if it's a starter and around twice that amount if it's the main course.
- Pâté as an appetiser: Figure on 50 g and one slice of toast cut into four triangles per person (plus a few spare slices).
- Seafood as an appetiser: Allow around 30 g of shelled seafood per person; 1 kg of prawns should make about 16 prawn cocktails.
- Meat or poultry as a main course: These days nutritionists say we should eat far less meat, so allow a maximum of 250–300 g per person if it is meat on the bone, but half that if it is boneless

(bearing in mind that some hearty eaters mightn't approve).

- Fish as a main course: ½ kg of fish (with head and tail) should serve two people comfortably; allow 150–200 g of fillets per person.
- Rice or pasta as an accompaniment: Allow around 45–50 g uncooked rice or pasta per person.

* One of the best ways of entertaining and knowing you're not going to waste food (or money) is a buffet. Prepare large quantities of a select few dishes. Small serving dishes are easier to heat than large ones and then you can line both sides of the table so you can have two queues going at once. Keep an eye on what's happening — any leftovers can be refrigerated for the next day or, if the dish hasn't even made it to the table, frozen for another time.

## TRAVEL

* If breakfast is part of your accommodation package, eat up big and save on the cost of lunch.

* Do your travelling off-peak and you'll find cheaper fares. Don't fly during school holidays and other popular travelling times if possible. Planning a weekend interstate? Try to organise a Friday and Monday off to make it a long weekend and you should make a saving on the fare. Book your flights well in advance for the best deals and always ask what's available.

* APEX air fares equal a 60 per cent saving, excursion fares are up to 45 per cent, advance purchase is around 35 per cent and stand-by is around 20 per cent discount.

* Going without travel insurance is not a saving. If something is going to go wrong, then it's bound to be around holiday time, and depending where you are, it will be very expensive to fix — much more than the outlay on insurance. Make sure, however, that you shop around rather than just taking what the travel agent offers you; it may be better to talk to an insurance company directly.

* When you're booking a family holiday, look for the little extras. Free child care is becoming common practice. Make sure your hotel offers it so you and your partner can have a break without the kids. Many hotels offer free activities for children. Why book into one with tennis courts if you have to pay $10 per game? Consider asking for a family apartment. Many hotels now offer these, and a kitchenette will save time and money when there are children whose appetites don't match what's on the menu.

* Always buy package holidays when you're planning a holiday which will require hotel accommodation. You'll get a better buy than buying air tickets and hotel accommodation separately.

* Remember, a waterfront hotel is always more expensive than one a few streets back from the beach. If it's only a short walk, is the view worth the price difference?

* Caravan parks have had to lift their game to stay in the race. You don't need to tow your own as most have on-site vans or cabins at competitive prices. These days, too, they often offer many of the facilities that a full resort does — playgrounds, pools, games rooms, barbecues, shops and special entertainment during holiday periods — and if the budget is tight, they can be a

very viable alternative. Plus, you don't have to stay in one spot if your inclination is to keep on travelling.

* Alternative considerations for cheap holidays are bed and breakfast establishments (many are wary of children under 10), farm stays, or hostel accommodation. Contact the Youth Hostel Association (family memberships are available) in your nearest capital city for details on membership costs and a copy of the YHA Australia-wide accommodation guide.

# HEATING, COOLING AND LIGHTING

## SAVING ENERGY

For any information on improving energy use, visit the Energy Information Centre in your nearest capital city or contact your state government Department of Minerals and Energy. You can also write to the National Building Technology Centre (PO Box 310, North Ryde NSW 2113) for pamphlets on energy efficiency and the science of building. You could also ask for advice at your local gas and electricity showrooms.

## BUILDING VALUE

* Building a new home? Check out the possibilities of making it a solar passive design, siting it to take best advantage of the prevailing winds and the movements of the sun. You can save a huge amount of money on heating and cooling costs.
* Check the position of windows and doors to allow for a cross-flow of air. If you have a choice, build on a concrete slab rather than on stumps, as there's less heat loss. And think twice about slab heating: toasty floors might sound like a great idea but this form of heating can be very expensive and not as efficient as a good natural covering.
* Design your floor plan so rooms are easy to shut off for more efficient heating and cooling. If you've opted for an open-plan home with archways rather than doors, perhaps you could fit curtains for use in winter only.
* Insulation is a must to preserve the climate you want inside your home. The initial outlay may seem steep but consider that 15 to 20 per cent of heat is lost through the walls of an uninsulated house and close to 40 per cent through the roof. Outlaying money on good insulation material will save dollars in the long run.
* With new homes or old, take a closer look at your windows. Up to 20 per cent of

heat is lost through expanses of glass, so think again about curtains or some form of window covering (floor-length curtains offer the best insulation). If you like the look of open space and big windows, investigate the cost of double glazing. Remember, too, that depending on which direction your windows face, they could also absorb a great deal of unwanted heat during the summer — another reason to invest in some type of covering. And once you've spent money on the coverings, remember to keep them closed at the appropriate time.

• Check the seals around doors and windows and recaulk when necessary. Heat loss may be small but it's constant and soon mounts up. And consider investing in several of the old-fashioned fabric-and-sand door snakes to shut off drafts from under the door.

## POWER PLANTING

• Watch what you plant and where. By planting deciduous plants around your house, you can reduce your energy bills.

They can provide shade in summer and reduce the amount of heat reflected from the ground, while allowing winter sun into the house.

• Trees can also be used to deflect breezes into the house during summer or block them in winter — check the prevailing winds in your area.

• Also be careful that trees do not shade your solar power collectors.

## AIRCONDITIONING

• If you have an airconditioning unit, make sure it's not running when the house is empty.

• And if you are running an airconditioning unit, set it at a comfortable and medium 18–21 degrees Celsius and keep filters and vents clean and operating efficiently.

• One of the simplest and prettiest ways of airconditioning a room is simply to use a large bowl under an open window — evaporation works wonders. Use several large round goldfish bowls and add some soil and water plants and you've got a cheap and attractive form of airconditioning as soon as there is any sort of draft.

## BEDDING

• Electric blankets cost money to operate. If you must have one, use it simply to heat the bed and then turn it off once you get in. You'll feel much better in the morning if you don't cook yourself overnight.

• Or buy a good doona and sleep directly under it as they do in Europe, rather than under a sheet and doona as we tend to do here. A couple of pretty doona covers changed regularly with the sheets and pillowslips is less expensive than constant bills for the electric blanket.

• Still cold? Invest in some old-fashioned flannelette sheets, bedsocks, and a hot water bottle — much cheaper and much cosier!

## ELECTRICAL APPLIANCES

• When you're in the market for a new electrical appliance, check the Energy Rating label: the lower the energy consumption figure, the greater the number of stars on the label and the more you'll save in running costs. If there isn't a label, talk to the dealer and evaluate all the information you can get before you make your final decision.

• Don't use the hair drier unless you absolutely have to. It's healthier to dry your hair naturally and you're saving money. If you do have to use one, use it on a low setting. It's the air that's doing the drying rather than the temperature, which can also cause damage. Using the highest setting is going to cost the most money.

• Don't keep the TV or radio running if you're not actually watching or listening. You're paying for power that isn't being used and although it may seem like a small amount, it does add up.

• When using the vacuum cleaner, empty the dust bag regularly. The machine will work more efficiently, which saves you time and money.

• Boiling the kettle? Use cold water and only boil the amount you need at the time.

• Don't automatically buy an electric gadget. There may be a perfectly good manual version that will do the job as well.

• See also Dishwashers and Whitegoods, in the chapter General Money-Saving Tips.

## HEATING

### WOOD FIRES AND POT BELLY STOVES

• Choosing the right form of heating can be difficult. Wood fires may look terrific and seem romantic, but they're not particularly efficient and can be very expensive if you don't have access to a free supply of wood and have to buy it instead.

• Consider a pot-belly stove instead of a wood fire; they're a much more efficient user of wood, and offer better heating.

• If you are using an open fire or pot-belly stove for your heating needs, try buying wood when it's cheaper, such as during the spring and summer, rather than in the winter when it's in demand and probably more expensive. If you have friends in the country and they have abundant wood, try to bring back a load — with their blessing — if you spend a weekend with them.

## ELECTRIC OR GAS

- Electric heaters are also quite expensive to run. If you have a choice, consider gas room heaters. The initial outlay may seem expensive but piped gas is a reasonably cheap and highly efficient heat source. Plan to buy your heater at the end of the winter or just before the next cold season if possible; there's every chance of new models replacing old ones, and great savings can be had on the superseded models.

## KEEPING THE HEAT

- Any form of heater needs regular maintenance to work at its best and most cost-efficient. Dust or vacuum the unit regularly because dust will impede air flow and circulation. Have major heating appliances checked regularly by a professional, perhaps every second year.
- Investigate the possibility of fitting timer switches to whatever heat source you use. You can set them to come on just before you get up, or just before you're due home, and to turn off when you leave or go to bed.
- When you do have a heater running, make sure any cupboards in the immediate area are closed; they don't need to be heated but they will soak up the warmth. And if you're using a bathroom or kitchen exhaust fan with the heater on, turn the

fan off as soon as you've finished in the area or you could drain all the warm air out very quickly.

• And don't immediately reach for the heater's 'on' switch when you feel cold: toss on a sweater and a warmer pair of socks, or maybe a tracksuit. You'll probably feel warm enough immediately, and you'll save on power costs.

• Do you have ceiling fans for keeping the house cool in summer? Turn them on during the winter; they'll spread warm air around the house too.

## HOT WATER

• You can reduce the size of your hot water bills, be they gas or electricity, by insulating the storage tank and pipes. Use mineral wool insulation on the tank and foam rubber tubes on the pipes. Ask your plumber for other suggestions.

• And make sure the system is sited in a spot where it is least affected by cold weather. It will have to work harder to heat the water if it is unprotected, and that means a greater cost to you.

• Consider resetting the thermostat of your hot water service. Chances are it is set quite high, which costs money to maintain. Turn it down several degrees, perhaps to 50–55 degrees Celsius. It will be hot enough for all your needs and, importantly, if there are young children or old people in the house, there is less risk of scalding. Discuss this with your plumber.

• If you're installing a new hot water service and you don't have access to gas, consider an off-peak system which will heat during the times when electricity is cheaper. Or think about a solar water heater. We live in a country with plenty of sunshine — harness some of this free form of energy to work for you.

**KEEPING COOL**

• Use cold water to do as many household chores as you can. For example, fill the kettle with cold water, wash down the bench with a sponge wrung out in cold water and wash your hands in cold water with a little hot added rather than hot water with some cold added. Anything that uses less power means less cost at bill time.

• When running the tap to get hot water, don't just let the cold run down the drain. Collect it in a jug to water the indoor plants, or in the kettle for your next cup of tea.

• Shut off the water heater when you're away for a weekend or longer. Not only does it save you money because you're not paying to maintain a comfortable water temperature when you don't need it, but it's also safer.

**CLEAN SAVINGS**

• Take shorter showers and consider shutting the water off, or down to a trickle, while you're lathering up so you don't waste hot water.

• If you've decided to treat yourself to a relaxing bath, do so, but don't fill the bathtub up to the top. It holds a lot of water and that's money down the drain. Keep an eye on the temperature. Run the taps equally so you keep it at a comfortable temperature right from the start, rather than running a steaming hot bath and then having to wait till it cools before you can get into it.

## LIGHTING

• Cut your lighting costs by using clear globes instead of pearl ones. It means you can use a lower wattage to produce the same amount of light and a lower wattage means lower cost.

- Dust your bulbs and light fittings regularly.
- Light-coloured walls reflect light better than dark-coloured ones, so if the room is due for a paint job, keep it light.
- Pale-coloured lampshades allow more light out than dark ones. Make sure the shade is kept dust-free too.
- Install power switches with dimmers. They work well for romantic dinners or for a child who's scared of the dark, and a dimmed light is cheaper to run.
- Fluorescent lights are cheaper to run than incandescent bulbs; they produce a similar amount of power for around 25 per cent of the energy (and cost). They also last longer, which is another saving. Fit them in areas where you need good light - the kitchen, the laundry, the workshop - and make sure children have a fluorescent lamp on the desk for homework rather than one with an ordinary bulb.
- Save your high-wattage bulbs (if you aren't using fluorescents) for areas where you're working and use low-wattage ones in hallways and the second toilet. If you are using incandescent bulbs for work areas, switch to the reflector type: they're more efficient.
- Get into the habit of switching off lights when you leave a room and teach your children the same habit. Why pay for power that isn't being used?
- Do you really need to leave an outdoor light on all night? If you are going out for the evening, perhaps you could consider installing the sensor type which comes on as you approach. They're also a handy security aid if you are at home — you'll know if someone is coming to the door.

## SOLAR POWER

- Have a very serious think about solar power. You may find there are incentives for going solar — talk to your local council or Building Information Centre.
- It may be possible to have a system that caters for most of your needs apart from cooking, and that will be comparable in cost terms to the more usual systems. Or you might look at a smaller system to operate in conjunction with the normal power supply. This perhaps could run outside lighting, the swimming pool filter and any ceiling and exhaust fans.
- Using solar energy means less dependence on fossil fuels, which is better for the environment and your wallet.

# SAVING MONEY WITH YOUR CAR

## BUYING CARS

**WHAT ARE YOU LOOKING FOR?**

• Whether you buy a new car or a used one, decide exactly what you need it for and buy the most appropriate model for the job. The trend towards 4WD is an expensive one, and most of the off-road vehicles currently registered will never go off-road. There are other types of cars which can carry plenty of passengers or tow heavy items, without the extra expense of running a 4WD. So, as with anything else, why pay for what you don't need? Find the size and shape model that suits your needs, and consider fuel economy as an important factor.

• When buying a car, either new or used, remember that the game — and it is a game — involves the salesperson trying to get you to pay as much as possible. That may mean you are urged to take the one on the floor instead of ordering one in the colour you want, the addition of a number of expensive options, or more expensive dealer finance and insurance. You, obviously, are interested in paying as little as possible for exactly what you want, with the best deal in terms of finance and insurance, so you're on opposite sides. Keep that in mind and do your homework first. No matter what salespeople promise, no matter how helpful they seem, if the deal isn't good for you, they shouldn't get the business. The last thing you need is to leave a showroom, or a private seller, having handed over a lot of hard-earned cash in return for something you don't really want or aren't really sure about.

**NEW CARS**

When buying a new car, consider the interior as well as the exterior. A cloth-trimmed interior (rather than vinyl or leather) will be warmer in winter and cooler in summer, which might save on energy diverted into heating or airconditioning. If there's a baby or youngster in the family and vinyl seems like a practical consideration in terms of cleaning up regurgitated milk or chocolate scraps, consider going with the vinyl but investing in some fabric car seat covers which are easily washable but still provide the same comfort level.

**USED CARS**

* If you're buying a used car, you could save yourself a lot of money by getting an inspection done of your proposed purchase by the technical department of your state's motoring organisation. They'll pick up any problems which might cause you expensive trouble later on, or problems which would suggest you look at another vehicle.

* For a guide to prices, if you're buying privately, check out comparable models at a reputable dealer.

**WHAT TO READ**

The best investment first off is to buy a copy of Universal Magazines' two bibles: Tony Davis's *The New Car Buyers Guide* and Ewan Kennedy's *The Used Car Buyers Guide*. For less than $10 from your newsagent, they will answer a lot of questions.

## GETTING AROUND

* When planning to head out and about, organise your time to do as many things as possible on the one trip, and plan it so you're not backtracking or, if possible, not

driving in peak-hour traffic. You'll save wear and tear on the car, and in petrol, and in your time, which is money, too.

- And if you can avoid the car — walking to the shops or the station to catch your train — do so. It's the ultimate way to save on all types of car costs. Use public transport or invest in a bicycle and ride wherever you have to go.
- Drive at a normal rate of speed for true savings in petrol costs. Driving fast makes the car work harder and boosts fuel use heavily. Driving too slow has the same effect. Generally, if you drive at advised speeds, change gears and brake smoothly and correctly, you'll get the most efficient use from your engine and your petrol dollar.
- Switch your engine off if you're caught in a traffic jam.
- Another aspect of fuel economy: don't carry around what you don't actually need each day; excess weight means excess fuel usage. Make sure there is only the bare minimum in the boot, such as the spare tyre (properly pumped up) and tool kit, and leave the roof racks off unless you need to use them that day.
- If you drive to work regularly and live in an area close to fellow workers, think carefully about a car pool. You'll save money by sharing the cost of petrol, and wear and tear on the car if you take it in turns with each other's car. Consider the following figures regarding the amount of fuel used per person to cover the distance to work:

Large car:
  1 person — 6 km/L per person
  4 people — 24 km/L per person
Small car:
  1 person — 9 km/L per person
  4 people — 35 km/L per person
Bus: 50 people — 50 km/L per person
Train: 300 people — 55 km/L per person

# RUNNING COSTS

- Buy the fuel type that's recommended for your car. And if you're buying a new car, think twice if it's a model that relies on a high-octane fuel: that can make for expensive running. Most cars will run well on high octane, but if they run just as well on lower octane, it's an obvious saving.
- Make sure your car is tuned regularly and the spark plugs are clean to ensure efficient petrol use. A full service and tune-up twice a year could save up to 20 per cent on your annual fuel bill.
- A manual car uses 10 per cent less petrol than an automatic.
- Keep a careful eye on your tyres. Incorrect pressures damage tyres and can result in their needing replacement earlier than necessary, as well as increasing petrol consumption. And underinflated or overinflated tyres can also cause accidents.
- Learn to change your car's oil yourself and collect the oil in a container and recycle it. Check with your local service station or your state pollution control centre on where oil collection centres are. Car batteries and old tyres also can be recycled.
- Is there build-up of film on the inside of the windscreen and you've run out of window cleaner? Rub over it with the cut edge of a potato and buff dry with a soft cloth.
- When the mechanic tells you the car needs a new part, try a nearby wrecker. Chances are you can get a perfectly good replacement second-hand for a lot less than a brand-new one. This is true from engines to window-winders. Talk to your mechanic.

- Speaking of mechanics, you'll save yourself a lot of time and money if you cultivate your relationship with a good mechanic. This is the person you can rely on to be honest with you, and that will save you money. Ask for recommendations from friends and take the time to find a good one. Once your car is out of warranty and you no longer need to rely on the dealer's service department, you could do yourself a real favour by finding a local operator.

- Instead of expensive car deodorants, sprinkle a few drops of essential oil on a tissue or cottonwool ball and place it inside the air vent or slightly open ashtray. Citrus oils help freshen stale air, while basil or peppermint will help you stay awake when driving long distances.

## SAFETY

- Consider investing some money in doing an advanced driving course with a reputable school. You'll learn how to drive more smoothly, which will obviously save money in terms of fuel economy and wear and tear on the car, as well as learning skills to keep you away from an accident or out of trouble if one comes your way and you can't avoid it.

We're talking about saving lives. The added bonus is that these days some insurance companies will give discounts to people who've completed these courses because surveys show they do reduce accident rates — and that's a money saver, not only in insurance premiums, but also in terms of time and money lost through you or your car being off the road and in need of repair.

* One of the most common, and most costly, 'accidents' is a nose-to-tail crash. It's generally no accident: the person who hits is a driver who is too close to the car in front and that's carelessness, foolishness or plain lack of awareness.

* Learning to be truly aware while you're in a car, and realising that it takes full concentration to be in charge of all this hard steel in the middle of lots of soft human beings, will ultimately save a lot of money. Very few of us avoid being in at least one accident in our lives, and car crashes cost money.

# FINANCIAL FASHION

## CHIC BARGAINS

- Many of the top local (and overseas) designers have regular clearance sales at which you will find some real bargains, and style to boot!

- Ring the head office of the companies whose clothes you like and ask if they have a mailing list. That way you'll be notified of the where and when of any sales. This is the time to buy your classic staples at reasonable prices.

- Check also whether they have a regular factory outlet. Most of the big clothing companies do, and you can save a great deal of money on samples, seconds and ends of runs. With many stores, though, you'll need to check constantly because stock turns over so regularly. Once you find a factory outlet you like, get into the habit of popping in on a regular basis to keep an eye out for bargains.

- Remember to check their opening hours. A phone call to make sure they're open before you head on out could save time and money. A phone call is also a good idea if you want to double-check that they have the sort of stock you're after.

## RECYCLING FASHION

- Clearing out the cupboards? Obviously organisations such as opportunity shops and charities are always in the market for good used clothes, but if they're in very good nick (or it's a fashion mistake you've bought and never worn) and you're in need of cash, consider selling them through one of the many recycled fashion stores that have sprung up over the last few years. Most will sell customers' clothes on consignment, taking a percentage of the selling price, but a few dollars in the pocket are better than none.

- These same recycled fashion stores are also good spots to track down some real designer-label bargains for yourself, as many of them will stock local and overseas designers' samples and seconds, along with the cast-offs (some unworn) of our more well-heeled sisters and brothers.

- But before you consign a garment for sale or toss it out, look at it again. Could it be cut down easily into tailored shorts, or a collarless shirt, or a miniskirt from a maxi?

## NEW USES FOR CLOTHES

• If you are tossing out, remove the zippers and buttons first: they may come in handy when a zip breaks or you lose a button from another favourite garment. And don't just toss them in the bin. Think about whether you could use them as rags, or to cover coathangers to make padded hangers for good jackets. Or you might even take up the old-fashioned craft of patchwork and turn some of your old favourites into a family heirloom quilt.

• Don't just toss out old stockings and pantihose. Use them as strainers for used cooking oil and make your own soap, or reuse the oil for cooking. Or use them to cover a glass jar for sprouting bean shoots, to tie up climbing plants, or to store onions and garlic (knot between each bulb).

• Old jumpers can find myriad ways to reappear — and save you money. Unravel them, straighten the wool (wind around a bottle filled with hot water) and rewind ready for a knitting or crochet attack. A baby's sweater could become a tea cosy, oven mitt or cover for a hot water bottle with the appropriate adjustments. The sleeves of a sweater could become a pair of warm slippers. Or cut old jumpers into squares, bind the edges and use the results as pot holders, as polishing rags, for stuffing cushions or for making into a patchwork rug.

## CLOTHING CARE

• Try to buy clothes that are easy-care and require a minimum of handling. If they're drip-dry you save on power for the iron; if they're washable, you'll save a fortune on dry-cleaning.

• And many items which suggest they should only be dry-cleaned can be handwashed or even washed in the gentle cycle of your machine, but make sure you hang them to dry rather than putting them in the drier.

• Plan your clothes shopping sprees like any other form of shopping — and make a list. Check what's already in the wardrobe and work out whether you need an entire new outfit, one item, or just some new accessories. Accessories can be a cheap way of making an older-style outfit look up to date.

• Make sure you wash out your swimming costume after each use. Salt water and chlorinated water, if left alone, will shorten the life of the outfit.

• Taking proper care of your shoes will extend their life. Keep them well polished, and make sure the heels and soles are in good condition. When buying shoes, try to buy a pair that will go with several outfits. Then you can get by with just a few pairs instead of having a cupboard that looks like that of famous shoe fancier Imelda Marcos.

## KIDS' CLOTHES

The one sure thing about children is that they grow, so maybe it's not such a great idea buying brand-new clothes for the youngsters in your life. Consider checking out the local second-hand shop to take care of your infant or toddler, and check with your local school — chances are there is a second-hand uniform shop on the premises. There are even shops that specialise in kids' seconds, samples and already worn garments, much like the adult version. Check in your local newspaper or the phone book, or a bargain shoppers' guide.

# FOOD AND COOKING

See the section on entertainment in the chapter Wine, Dine, Have Fun and Travel for more tips about food and cooking.

## MEAT, FISH AND POULTRY

• Having trouble starting the barbecue? Don't bother with those expensive and perhaps toxic firelighters. Keep a supply of fat scraps in a container in the fridge and toss a few on the paper and twigs, then add a match.

• Cooking a curry or a casserole? Use less meat and fill out the dish with rice, potatoes, beans, lentils or extra vegetables.

• If you buy expensive meat such as fillet steak, ask your butcher to trim the fat before he weighs it. That way your top dollar buys only the best.

• If you buy cheaper meat, enhance it. Experiment with marinades — plan ahead to allow the meat to marinade overnight — or cut it finely and cook slowly to tenderise it.

• One tablespoon of vinegar added to a stew will make the meat more tender.

• If the steak is tough, pour 3 tablespoons of salad oil and 1 tablespoon of vinegar into a soup plate and soak the steak for half an hour, then turn it and soak for another
half-hour. Now you can cook your freshly tenderised steak.

• Whatever meat you use, serve less of it. You'll save money and the family will be healthier. Check with a nutritionist, a good cookbook or your doctor as to the optimum amount of meat per day; most of us eat far too much.

• To prevent a chicken sticking to the baking dish when roasting it, add a few drops of vinegar to the dripping. It doesn't affect the flavour.

• Making a meat loaf? If you think there'll be more than the family can eat at a sitting, slice the rest after cooking and put it into tomorrow's lunches, or remove some of the mix and bake a few small loaves in patty pans for lunches.

• Buy large cuts of meat — it's usually cheaper that way — and prepare several meals at once. For example, separate the side of lamb into appropriate meal-size proportions, label and freeze. If a particular cut is on special in bulk, do a double quantity of your favourite casserole or spaghetti sauce and freeze it.

* Cooking a whole chicken or a whole fish? Save the bones and other sundry bits and pieces and cook them up to make your own healthy full-flavoured stock. Freeze it till you need it, or freeze the 'bits' until you have time to make the stock.

* Dip mint in vinegar before chopping to make mint sauce and it will keep its bright green colour.

## DAIRY PRODUCTS

* Running out of butter? Beat in some fresh milk, which will not only make the butter go further but help reduce the proportion of animal fat in your diet. Simply soften the butter a little, then put into the blender and turn on the motor; pour the milk in a thin stream through the top. Watch the mixture carefully and turn off at the first sign of curdling. You can use as much as 100 mL of milk per 150 g of butter.

* Cheese dried out or gone mouldy in the fridge? Don't throw it out as it will still be useful in cooking. Allow it to dry out completely and cut off any mould, then grate it finely or process to a fine powder in a food processor or blender. Store in an airtight jar in the fridge.

* If your cheese has gone mouldy but there's too much to process, don't worry. The mould is not a harmful variety. Trim away the surface mould and wipe the cheese over with a clean cloth soaked in strong salty water. Allow the surface to dry out at room temperature for a short time, then put the cheese into a clean, dry container and return to the fridge. Not only have you regenerated the cheese for another day, the salt solution will inhibit the growth of more mould.

* If there's a special on cheese, and it's a bargain too good to miss but you don't have enough room in the fridge, simply dip it in melted candle wax, or pour the wax over it. The cheese can be stored in the pantry this way for several weeks. Crack the wax and remove when you're ready to eat the cheese, and then store it in the fridge.

* Extend your whipped cream and reduce your fat intake in one easy move. For each small bottle of cream you've whipped, whip one egg white until bulky but still moist and then fold this gently into the cream to extend it.

* Plain yogurt is generally cheaper than flavoured, and you can flavour your own with your favourite tinned or fresh fruit.

* The recipe calls for sour cream but you only have real cream and the shops are shut? Simply add a dessertspoon of vinegar to the cream and you have some instant sour cream.

* Does the recipe call for buttermilk? Cultured buttermilk is available from some supermarkets and health food shops but making your own version may be cheaper. A good substitute is plain yogurt mixed with low-fat milk. Or use sour milk which you can make by adding 1 tablespoon of vinegar or lemon juice to 1 cup of ordinary milk. (This is particularly good when making scones or pikelets.)

* Whipping cream for filling layer cakes? Add a small pinch of bicarbonate of soda and the cream will stay fresh for days.

## FRUIT AND VEGETABLES

• Are oranges available in bulk but the whole family is off orange juice? Turn it into marmalade and freeze the excess in old takeaway food tubs. Turn it into sorbet for a refreshing dessert, or freeze it in suitable containers as nutritious ice blocks for the small fry. Or simply cut the oranges into slices and freeze as ice blocks for the children or as garnish for summer drinks.

• Are lemons available in bulk but you can't use them all at once? Same deal as above: squeeze them and freeze the juice. Check your recipes and see what they ask for and freeze the juice in containers that match the required quantities. Or simply fill ice-cube trays with the juice. Measure the quantity of water that makes one cube to give you an idea of how many cubes you'll need for your recipes when you're cooking.

• Making mashed potatoes? Don't add cream or milk, which cost in terms of cents and kilos, just use some of the water you cooked the potatoes in.

• Making your own jam can be an expense rather than a saving if you're doing it in

**THE ULTIMATE BOOK OF MONEY HINTS** ■ **37**

small batches. Given the cost of ingredients and your time, it's probably cheaper to buy the same type from the supermarket. However, if you've got a large supply of containers and you get the fruit free (from your own fruit trees or those of a neighbour), it may be well worth the effort. Mind you, it's hard to calculate the cost-saving or the expense if the actual exercise of making the jam is therapeutic!

• Passionfruit is another fruit to buy in bulk when it's cheap and freeze. Place whole ones into the freezer as picked; they will keep for at least 12 months and taste quite fresh when thawed. Or scrape the pulp into ice-cube trays and freeze, storing the cubes in plastic bags once frozen.

• Making a date loaf? Soak the dates overnight in cold tea to improve their flavour.

## EGGS

• If there's a special on eggs that you want to take advantage of, do so: they can be stored for a long time in the fridge. To extend that storage time, wipe the shells with olive oil or petroleum jelly to prevent air getting in to spoil them.

• Make sure they're not sitting next to anything strong-smelling because they will absorb odours: keep cheese, fish or onions in sealed containers away from the eggs.

• Test for freshness by putting the egg into a basin of cold water; if it floats, it's bad and shouldn't be used.

• Always crack eggs into a cup, one at a time, when cooking. That way you'll immediately know if one is bad, rather than ruining the entire recipe mix and having to start again.

• Put a teaspoon of vinegar in the saucepan when poaching eggs to prevent the yolks breaking and to keep the whites snowy.

## A SEVEN-DAY MENU

• Save money on your weekly food bill by planning a seven-day menu. Then you know exactly what you need to buy when you do the shopping and things won't go unused and need to be thrown out.

• If you've done this and an unexpected dinner invitation arrives, try to reshuffle your eat-at-home menu. Perhaps you can still cook the casserole you were planning and freeze it, rather than trying to work out what to do with some tired meat at the end of the week.

## LEFTOVERS

• It's also a good idea to consider things you can do with leftovers so they can be properly reused rather than thrown out or fed to the dog.

• If there are favourite meals your family likes to eat regularly and there are leftovers from those meals each time, have a good think about ways to reuse them, or a more efficient way of cooking so there aren't leftovers.

• If the only possibility is to throw them out, think first of the compost bin rather than the garbage bin.

• Leftover tea and coffee have an alternative life to going down the drain or into the compost bin: simply freeze the dregs in ice-cube trays and then add them to iced tea or coffee in the summer. It means the refreshing drink you're enjoying won't be diluted as the ice melts.

- If the recipe calls for 1 tablespoon of tomato paste but the sachet holds more, don't throw out the leftover amount. Simply package it up in measured quantities of 1 tablespoon, wrap in plastic wrap and freeze. Pull out of the freezer the next time you need a small amount.

## SPECIAL TREATS

- Want exotic ice cream or sorbet for dessert? Make your own. Use your imagination in choosing your ingredients and you'll enjoy the dessert even more because you know what pure ingredients have gone into the mix. You don't have to buy an electric ice-cream maker, although if you enjoy ice cream, they're a good investment.

- Make the kids' ice blocks. Buy the appropriate trays or plastic moulds and fill them with fruit juice (home-squeezed or bought) or the syrup from canned fruit diluted with water.

## PLAN AHEAD

- Watch out for the catch in pre-packaged food, be it meat or fruit or vegetables — it's not a bargain if it's more than you need or can utilise at the time. If you can't cook and freeze the extra (or store it in some way), chances are you'll end up throwing some out, and that's no saving. There's also the possibility that the good stuff on the top is covering up something less than desirable.

- Try to plan your meals in line with what fruit and vegetables are in season. It's always cheaper than buying something that's not in season and therefore exotically priced.

- To make some easy-to-store freezing containers, line ice-cream containers with good-sized freezer bags and place the casserole or sauce to be frozen in the container. Once it's frozen, remove from the container and just store the plastic-wrapped 'brick', but make sure it's labelled. For easier thawing and cooking in a saucepan or round microwave container, use a round container to do the freezing in, suitably lined with a freezer bag. This is a particularly good method for soup or spaghetti sauce, and you don't have every container you own tied up in the freezer.

- Whenever you're putting up food of any type, either for freezer or cupboard storage, remember to label and date it. Months later when you pull a packet of brown meat from the freezer or try to tell which jar holds which type of flour, you'll wish you had so you'd know what was what. Having the date on the package or jar also helps work out whether something is still useable or past its use-by date. Some foods age subtly and it's not always obvious to the naked eye whether they're still useable or not.

- Don't add new flour to old in the canister. Wholemeal flour contains natural oils which can turn rancid with time and ruin the fresh grain. Wash the container and refill, or put the new batch in a separate container, write on its use-by date and use up the older flour first.

- Weevils and moths can be a problem, particularly if you're buying grains, pulses or flour in bulk. When you bring the packages home, put them in the freezer for 48 hours before transferring them to the pantry cupboard (put paper flour bags into a plastic bag first). This should kill any eggs. Alternatively, put them in the microwave for 1 to 2 minutes on high (large packages may need to be opened and the contents spread out in a microwave-proof dish) or in the oven for 10 minutes on moderate. After either method, put the food, once it has come back to room temperature, into airtight storage jars to prevent any reinfestation from bugs which are already living in the pantry. Add a bay leaf for good measure. If there are already bugs in what you've bought, they're not harmful. Simply sieve to remove any developed insects and treat as above.

## PARTY FOOD

- Making something for a party and you need, or want, something special? Take a closer look at what you're serving. Fruit salad can look really attractive served in a scooped-out watermelon or pineapple skin and fruit sorbet is even more appetising when frozen in orange, lemon or cantaloupe skins (depending on the flavour).

- Having a dinner party and the funds have run out before you finalised something to have with coffee? How about fruit dipped in chocolate? Simply buy a block of cooking chocolate — or buy a small one each of ordinary milk, dark and white chocolate — and melt it. Skewer bite-sized fruit pieces with a toothpick, using strawberries, banana slices, brandied prunes or apricots, raisins and crystallised ginger. Then dip in the chocolate which has been allowed to cool a little. Set the coated pieces on a metal tray covered in freezer plastic which has been chilled in the freezer for a few minutes. When the tray is full, put it in the fridge to allow the chocolate to fully set. Then peel the chocolates off the plastic and arrange as desired.

- Leftover Christmas pudding also makes a great end-of-evening treat. Simply crumble into a bowl and pour on a generous slug of brandy (if children are involved, use fruit juice instead). Mix to the consistency of truffles, then take spoonfuls of the mix and shape into balls, placing them in rows on greaseproof paper set on a baking tray. Pop the lot in the freezer for several hours until they are very firm. Now spread some plastic wrap on a baking tray and chill for a few moments while you melt your cooking chocolate, again, perhaps a little of each colour. Remove the pudding drops from the freezer, spear each with a toothpick and fully dip in the warmed chocolate. Place each on the chilled tray and remove the toothpick immediately (wash fingers between every few chocolates). Decorate the tops immediately with a piece of crystallised fruit or a nut as they will set quickly.

## POTATO NESTS

* Even savoury food can be jazzed up in no-cost serving containers. Simply turn potato into potato nests, in which meat or seafood looks terrific and the container is edible.

* To make the nests you need two small metal sieves, one a little larger than the other, and a deep pan suitable for frying. Grate the raw potatoes and rinse them under cold, running water. Turn out onto a clean tea towel and pat dry. Heat some oil in the pan, then divide the potato into the number of portions you'll need. Spread the first portion in the large sieve and press the smaller one into it, which will compress the 'nest'. Dip the whole lot in the oil and fry until the potato is golden-brown. Turn the nest out onto absorbent paper and repeat with more grated potato until you have made enough. For appetisers, use two very small sieves or strainers.

# MAKING YOUR OWN

## DOG BISCUITS

Mix together 4 cups of wholemeal flour, 200 g good-quality minced meat and 2 teaspoons of salt. Add enough cold water to mix to a stiff dough. Roll out and place on an oven tray, mark into squares and prick several times with a fork. Bake in a slow oven until brown. If you have a puppy rather than a full-grown dog, add 1 tablespoon of cod liver oil as it is a bone-builder.

## FROMAGE FRAIS

When the recipe calls for fromage frais and the wallet is empty or the supermarket is closed, an acceptable substitute can be made by combining equal quantities of cottage cheese and yogurt with a squeeze of lemon juice. Whip in a blender or food processor to a fine consistency.

## MILK ICE BLOCKS

* These are a delicious treat for the kids, and they're good for them. Good for you, too!

* Warm 600 mL of fresh milk and add 4 tablespoons of powdered milk, sweetening with a dash of condensed milk to your liking. Beat until dissolved, then add 2 bananas sliced into small pieces and the pulp of 2 passionfruit. Pour into appropriate containers and freeze.

## SOFT CHEESE

* It seems a shame to throw out sour milk. It may have gone off quickly in the summer heat and if it means tossing the better part of the carton away, don't do it. The bacteria that have turned it sour are the same ones you need to make cheese.

* Make up the sour milk with fresh to about a litre in quantity. Leave it covered on the kitchen bench until it has set, which will only take a few hours in warm weather. Line a colander with a clean piece of sheet, muslin or cheesecloth and pile in the curdled milk. Tie this up in a bundle and hang it over a bowl in the fridge until it stops dripping. (Use the whey which has dripped out in place of all or some of the liquid mentioned in recipes for soups, casseroles, cakes, bread, mashed potato or

sauces.) Scrape the curds (which are cheese) into a bowl and flavour them. Add chopped fresh or dried herbs and a pinch or two of pepper, chilli, garlic salt or dried onions. Or make a fruit cheese: add chopped dried apricots, apples, sultanas and a dash of rum or brandy, plus a little nutmeg and honey to taste. Allow to harden a little more, then serve.

## SUNDRIED TOMATOES

*2 kg egg tomatoes, halved*

*2 sprigs rosemary or a handful of basil leaves*

*1 clove garlic, halved*

*1 cup olive oil*

Place the tomatoes, cut side down, on a wire rack over a baking tray and bake in a very slow oven for about 10 hours or until they have shrivelled and dried. Turn them during the drying process. Pack them in hot sterilised jars, add the herbs and garlic, pour in enough oil to cover the tomatoes completely, and then seal the jars. This recipe is not suitable for microwaving.

## TIA MARIA

*1 cup sugar*

*1 cup hot water*

*4 heaped teaspoons instant coffee*

*1 dessertspoon vanilla*

*1 cup underproof rum*

Dissolve the sugar and coffee in the hot water, then add the vanilla. Allow to cool, then add the rum. Bottle and allow to stand for a week before using.

## YEAST

* Make a paste of 3 tablespoons of plain flour mixed with 2 tablespoons of sugar and ½ cup of lukewarm water. Seal the mixture in an airtight jar and allow to stand in a warm place for about 48 hours. The fermented yeast is now ready to use.

* To keep it working, feed every other night with 2 tablespoons of flour, 1 tablespoon of sugar and 3/4 cup of lukewarm water mixed to a paste.

## YOGURT

*1.2 L warm water*

*12 tablespoons skim milk powder*

*5 tablespoons good-quality commercial yogurt (this is the starter)*

Turn the oven on to the lowest temperature. Put the water (a little warmer than blood heat) into a bowl and mix in the skim milk powder, whisking until it's smooth. Add the yogurt and mix well.

Warm six wide-necked glass jars by rinsing in hot water, then dry and fill them with the milk mixture. Place the jars on a tray and put them into the very slow oven, leaving them for 5 to 6 hours until the yogurt has set firmly. Seal the jars and store in the fridge.

A week's supply can be made this way at one time and stored in the fridge, but remember to save enough of the yogurt to start off your next batch.

Mix yogurt with honey, nuts or fruit of your choice.

# GOOD VALUE GARDENING

## GREEN THINKING

* Sick plants will respond to castor oil and water applied around their roots. Sick ferns will respond to a solution of ¼ cup of salt to 9 cups of lukewarm water.

* If you have a new garden and you haven't got around to planting it out fully, toss in some pumpkins, tomatoes or watermelons, things which grow easily with a minimum of fuss and give you an edible crop.

* An attractive and practical bird feeder can be made for very little cost. Simply hammer some galvanised nails around a block of timber at a 60-degree angle. Impale corncobs and apples on the nails. Add a hook at the bottom to hang a commercially bought seed ball and attract an even wider range of birds. Another hook or a metal ring at the top will enable you to hang the bird feeder from a tree in your garden. Replace the corncobs and apples when necessary.

* If you're planting a new lawn, consider sowing grasses that are tough and not so water-dependent. Talk to your local garden store. If you're planting a garden, consider native trees rather than exotics: natives are stronger and need less water.

* Save energy costs, and get some exercise, by using a hand mower. If you do use a power mower, don't run the mower at full speed, and never leave it running unattended. In both cases it's a waste of fuel, and in the second scenario, it's dangerous, particularly with children around.

* Did you know that tin cans and steel wool can help the soil in your garden? Tin cans are especially good for fruit trees. Crush them and spread them around the tree, then cover with around 20 cm of mulch. A year later they'll have decomposed, leaving a useful legacy. Used steel wool can simply be buried around the garden; hydrangeas love it: it makes the blue flowers a more vivid colour and the pink ones turn a pretty shade of mauve.

## PROPAGATION

* If you've got green fingers, cultivate seedlings or cuttings, plant them in a pretty pot and give them as gifts.

* African violets are reasonably simple to

propagate and make delightful gifts. The best time to strike leaves is between November and April during the warm weather. Cut off several matured leaves with a sharp knife, leaving 3.5 cm of stem on the leaf. Plant these leaves firmly in a pot, in a good potting mixture, covering the stem only. Keep them moist but not over-wet. Place the pot in a warm place out of draughts and direct sun. The shoots should start to appear in about two weeks. Take care not to overwater and always use tepid water, watering from the bottom by placing the pots in a saucer or shallow dish. Use a weak plant food solution occasionally. African violets like a bit of steam or humidity, so the bathroom and kitchen are good places to keep them.

- Save time and money by planting perennials, instead of annuals which need replacing each year, and self-seeding plants or ones that are easily struck from cuttings.
- Cardboard egg cartons make great propagation trays for seeds. Fill with soil and when the plants are ready, all you have to do is separate the individual cups, cut off the lower portion and plant, container and all. The cardboard will decompose. Or utilise toilet roll cylinders in a similar way by filling them with soil and standing them upright in an old ice-cream container. They too can be set out, container and all, when the plants are large enough.
- Another beaut idea for a seed box is an old suitcase. Fill it with soil and plant the seeds. Shut the lid at night to keep frost and pests away until the seedlings are hardy enough to be transplanted. This is an ideal use for a case with handles or locks missing.

## BANANAS

- Keep your staghorns happy and well fed by tucking a banana skin in at the back of the plant.
- Maidenhair ferns are banana fans too: chop up the skins and mix with their potting mix.
- See also the section Tea Leaves.

## INDOOR PLANTS

- Indoor plants respond well to a watering with either cold black tea or stale beer.
- Indoor plants also enjoy having their leaves washed over with one of the following: equal parts water and milk, equal parts water and beer, or a few drops of olive oil or glycerine on a soft cloth.

## FRUIT AND VEGETABLES

- Save money on fruit and vegetables by growing your own — and you don't need a huge garden to do it. Citrus trees will happily grow in pots, providing they're properly watered and fertilised, and will produce lots of fruit. Soft fruits such as berries, kiwi fruit and grapes will grow against a trellis in a narrow bed, as will peas, beans, pumpkin and rockmelon. And both vegetables and fruits will also grow happily in tubs or boxes or drums. Savour strawberries home-grown in a tub with holes cut into the sides and the plants poked in.
- Another possibility for cutting costs in the fruit and vegetable department is to investigate the wonders of hydroponics: growing greens with nutrient-packed

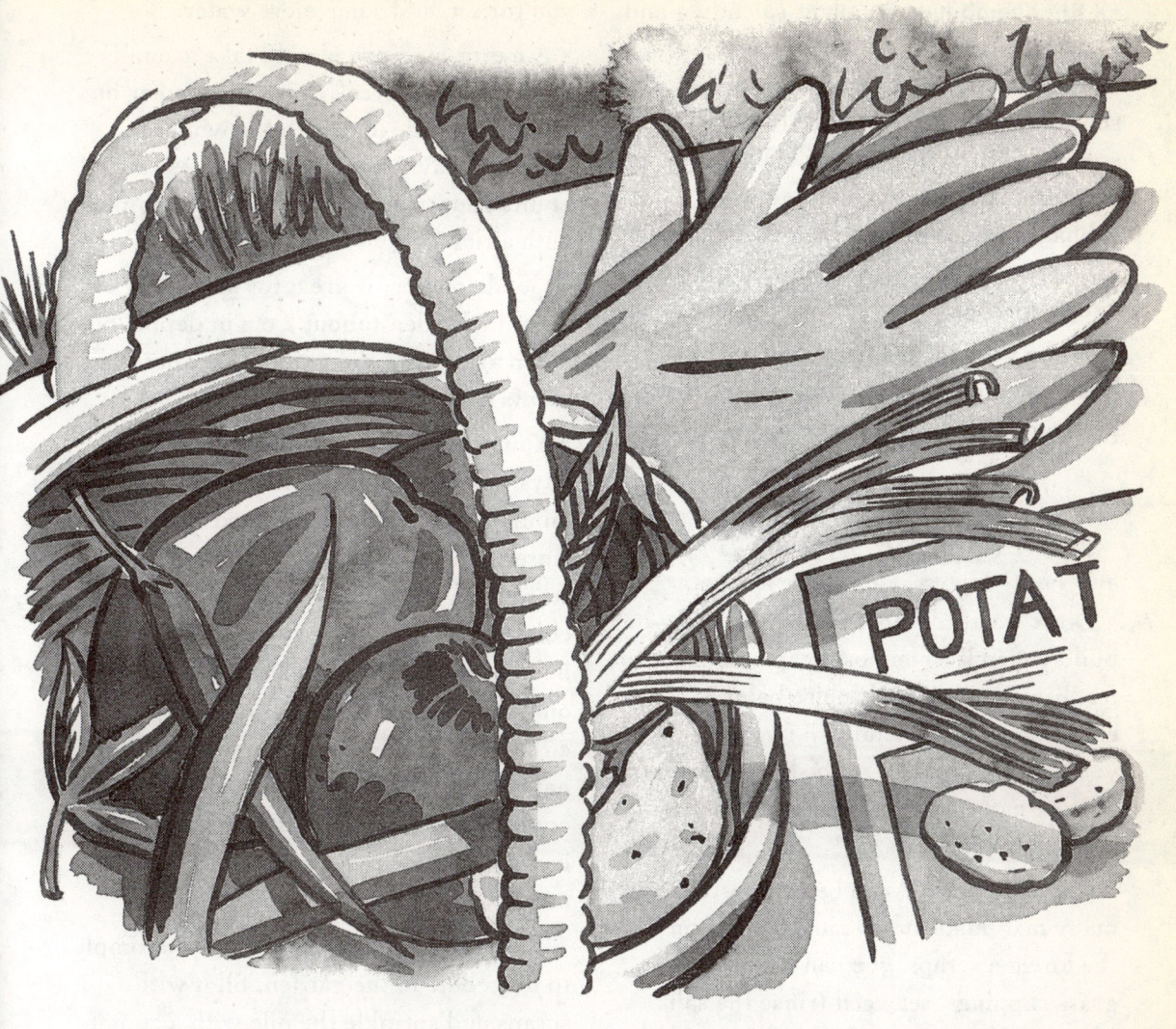

water. Specialist hydroponic shops are springing up all over the suburbs and you can buy anything from a very simple set-up for around $100 to something large and comprehensive. Lettuce does particularly well grown this way, so why not give yourself a wonderful summer salad mix, freshly home-grown with a minimum of fuss?

## COMPANION PLANTING

- As a really clever alternative to expensive and potentially environmentally damaging pest control, consider companion planting instead of spraying. Some plants act as natural pesticides so companion planting makes a lot of sense.

- Sage, rosemary, thyme and peppermints will deter slugs and cabbage butterflies, and lavender helps control ants and keeps aphids away from roses. French marigolds keep insects away, so plant them among your vegetables. Garlic and onion will control fungus diseases if planted around roses, fruit trees and strawberries. Nasturtiums keep woolly aphids away from fruit trees.

- Other combinations: plant calendula and tomato with asparagus to control asparagus beetle; plant eggplant, rosemary, rhubarb and marigolds with beans to control pea and bean weevils, blackfly and capsids; plant tomato and sage with cabbage to control cabbage caterpillar and cabbage root fly; plant basil with tomatoes to control flies.
- Talk to your local nurseryman or buy a book on companion planting and natural pest control for more information.

## COMPOSTING

- Don't waste all those kitchen scraps — build yourself a compost heap and use it to fertilise your garden. You're being environmentally friendly in two ways: you're taking up less rubbish tip space and putting natural products on the garden instead of chemicals.
- Anything natural can be composted, and many man-made items too. In addition to the kitchen scraps, you can use leaves, grass clippings, seaweed (rinse the salt off), rotted sawdust, wood ash, shredded paper, weeds, straw, the contents of the vacuum cleaner bag and floor sweepings.
- Clear a patch of ground and make sure it's level. Then place a few bricks around the edge to allow the air to circulate. Put your first layer in the middle of the square and dust over with a thin layer (about 1 cm) of chook or cow manure, dolomite or blood and bone and sprinkle with water. Repeat layers until your initial pile is built with whatever is immediately at hand. After a week, turn the pile over with a garden fork to speed up decomposition, and try to turn every two or three weeks after that. If the material is too dry when you turn it, add some more water.
- A metre-high pile should take around two months to break down in summer but will take a little longer in the winter. Consider having two or more piles started at different times to keep yourself supplied with a rich garden mix.
- Good compost is great for spreading over the garden (about 2 cm in depth) but it can also be used on its own for potting plants and raising seedlings.
- You can also buy compost bins these days, either from your environmentally minded local council or a good hardware store. You could consider building a tidier structure yourself using timber, bricks, concrete blocks or corrugated iron. It must be built on an earth floor and be open on one side for ease of access and air circulation. The other three sides need to have holes to help air circulation. If the contents look like spilling out, keep them in with a removable piece of fine wire mesh.
- The really easy way to compost is simply to dig a hole in the garden, fill it with scraps and sprinkle the pile with a cup of dolomite. Fill in the hole with the removed earth and wait a week or so. It will then be ready to spread around, or you can use the area as a planting spot for a new plant.
- If you want the compost to go further, turn it into a liquid fertiliser by adding about 10 cm of mature compost to a bucket of water. Let it stand for two days, stirred occasionally, then strain it through coarse cloth and water the needy plants with it. It's especially enjoyed this way by leafy vegetables.
- All these compost methods do several things. They help the garden, save you money on commercial fertiliser and potting

mix, and cut down on waste going into the garbage bin.

• There are some materials you should not add to your compost; burn them or put them in the rubbish bin. Don't use diseased plants or weeds with tough bulbs such as onion weed, oxalis and nut grass. Avoid plant materials such as eucalyptus leaves and pine needles which contain oils or resins and are very slow to break down, as are kitchen fats and greases. If you've treated your lawn with a weedkiller, don't add the clippings to the pile. High-carbon materials such as mature grass, straw, paper, sawdust and wood shavings should only be used in small amounts.

• Perennial weeds that might cause problems in the compost bin can be devitalised first. Simply put the weeds in a plastic bag and tie it, then leave them in a sunny corner of the garden for a few weeks before adding them to the compost heap — they won't regenerate. Or put them into a plastic bin and cover them with water. After several days you can pour this onto the compost pile.

- Lawn clippings should be allowed to dry out before adding them to the pile. Mix them well with other ingredients as they tend to mat together and become a slimy impenetrable mess.

## SPRAYS

- For tomatoes, lemons and roses with sooty mould, mix together 20 L of water, 2–3 cups of Epsom salts, 1 teaspoon of Condy's crystals and 1 teaspoon of white oil fungicide. Spray the foliage so it is well soaked and the mould should start to fall off after a few days.
- For aphids and thrips, mix ½ cup of Pine-O-Cleen eucalyptus disinfectant in 1 L of water. Spray the plants after rain or a good watering.
- For weeds, cut the leaves off a bunch of rhubarb, put them in a saucepan and cover with water. Add 1 or 2 bulbs of garlic, boil to a pulp and then strain. Let stand for 48 hours and then add the same amount of water to the strained liquid. Rhubarb leaves are poisonous so allow 14 days to elapse between spraying and harvesting if you are spraying vegetables or fruit.
- For snails, soak 100 g of chopped garlic in 2 tablespoons of liquid paraffin for 48 hours. Add 500 mL of water and 30 g of pure soap. Filter the mixture and store in a plastic container. To spray, add 3 teaspoons of the mixture to 1 L of water. This also works well on small sucking insects and soft-bodied larvae.
- To kill aphids, caterpillars and scale insects, you can use tobacco water. It is poisonous to humans so use it with care. Simply place 1 cup of tobacco into 4 L of warm water and leave to soak for 24 hours. You may wish to dilute this a bit more before spraying.
- For damping off fungus and powdery and downy mildew, put 1 cup of dried chamomile flowers in a ceramic bowl and top with 3 cups of boiling water. Cover and allow to sit overnight, then strain through a cloth, squeezing all liquid from the herbs.
- For mildews that attack the squash family, including zucchini, combine 1 cup of freshly chopped chives with 3 cups of boiling water in a ceramic bowl and allow to sit for 15 minutes before straining.

## TEA LEAVES

Tea leaves and cold tea work wonders in the garden. Here are a few ideas that will make use of old tea leaves and save on the cost of fertiliser and potting mix.

- Roses, violets, hydrangeas, azaleas, parsley and passionfruit vines all benefit from the dregs of a good cuppa. Loosen the soil and sprinkle the tea leaves around the base of the plants. With tea bags, leave to rot or allow the bag to dry and remove the leaves.
- Leftover tea and leaves are great for watering and mulching ferns, particularly the temperamental maidenhair. Don't smother the roots with leaves: simply dig in gently and allow air to circulate freely. Staghorns enjoy this treatment too.
- Add the leftover tea leaves and tea bags to the compost heap.
- Fill an old ice-cream container with tea leaves and then combine the leaves with half a container of soil and manure and use as a potting mix. Commercial potting mix blended with cold tea leaves makes a great seedbed.

- Before sweeping dusty paths or patios, sprinkle generously with damp tea leaves to help stop the dust rising.

## WATERING

- Watering a garden can sometimes seem like a major hassle when you're busy. Try doing it in the early hours of the morning or evening, using the time as your own quiet time, or consider using empty wine flagons or soft-drink bottles to do the watering instead. This method works very well with crops like melons or cucumbers which need a constant water supply. Simply fill the bottle with water and up-end it in the soil in the middle of a patch of vegetables. One bottle of water will last up to three days and can help prevent downy mildew. It's also a good way of making sure the water you use — and pay for — is going where it's needed and not being sprayed into the wind.

- A large proportion of your annual water bill goes into the garden. Save water and money by watering in early morning or evening to reduce the amount of water lost through evaporation.

- Mulch the soil around trees and shrubs

and on garden beds. This also prevents water loss through evaporation and so saves on water bills.

* Water the roots rather than the leaves to encourage deep root growth.
* Soaker hoses are the best way to water vegetable gardens which need a low-level spray. They're also particularly efficient for lawns and garden beds during very hot, dry or windy weather because they provide a light mist which soaks in well.
* If you handwash the dishes and use a pure soap to do so, then reuse the water on your plants. If you decide this is a long-term proposition with merit, perhaps you could talk to your plumber about the possibility of rerouting the run-off water to somewhere accessible. This could be to another tank, or a simple fitting on the downpipe from the sink might allow you to collect the run-off in a bucket.
* Think about installing a tank to collect rainwater run-off. This free water could be used for a multitude of purposes. Make sure you have a common-sized tap installed at the side of the tank that will connect with your hose fittings. Then you can easily water the garden, or wash the car, with water that isn't costing you a cent.

# GENERAL MONEY-SAVING TIPS

## HOME AND HEALTH HINTS

• Give up smoking: not only is it a costly habit to maintain but you'll save money on doctor's bills and dry-cleaning and washing costs.

• Use fabric handtowels and serviettes in preference to paper ones. If you must use paper ones, keep the lightly used ones in a bag under the sink and use them to wipe out pans or wipe up spills on the floor.

• Keep your steel wool from rusting by putting it in a plastic bag and keeping it in the freezer.

• Try to eat and entertain at home: it's cheaper than takeaway or restaurants. And take lunch to work as often as possible; once again, it's cheaper than buying it at the delicatessen across the road, and probably healthier.

• Cut back on using disposables: razors, tissues, lighters, paper plates and the like all add up. Washing and ironing handkerchiefs is less costly than buying and tossing away. It's also better for the environment.

• Consider making your own quilt cover instead of paying for an expensive one — you will often find two flat sheets at a cheaper price than the quilt itself. Simply stitch around three sides and use buttons and buttonholes, press studs or strips of velcro to close in the fourth side. You could even make a reversible quilt by using two different sheets. You could use two different colours, or have floral one side and checks or stripes the other. Make a set of matching pillow slips by buying slips to match each sheet. Slit through the seams and match one side in one colour or pattern to one side in the other colour or pattern and re-sew. Hey presto! You have matching pillowslips no matter which side of the quilt you use.

• Invest in a battery charger and re-charge all your small batteries (torch, transistor, alarm clock, camera) rather than buying

new ones regularly. Or give them an extra boost at the end of their useful lives by putting them in a warm oven for about an hour. They'll be good for another few hours' use.

• Save on storage hassles for winter quilts by using them as cushions in the family room. Simply fold your quilt into a manageable size, tuck some cloves into the middle, and sew a 'cushion cover' to fit. Or you could roll several together to use as a 'bolster' to turn a single bed into a couch. Again, make a cover to fit in an inexpensive and colour-coordinated fabric.

## SHOPPING

• Subscribe to a consumer magazine so you're in touch with what's happening and how you can get the best buy and avoid being ripped off.

• Heading out and about? Take only the money you'll need. You can't spend what you don't have, so a pocketful of change, or a few extra bills, won't end up disappearing with nothing substantial to show for them.

• Following the same line of action, leave your credit cards at home. If you carry them all the time, you will use them. Most of the time you know if you're going to need them, and if you are without them but see something you want, the trip home to collect them will give you time to have second thoughts about the purchase.

• Make a shopping list for every shopping trip you make: for groceries, for presents, for household purchases. It's too easy to see something and decide to get it purely on a whim. This mightn't be a problem if it's a packet of lollies that's not on the list, but if it becomes a more expensive Christmas or birthday gift than you'd originally planned, it can make a big hole in the budget.

* Take out a subscription to your favourite magazine or share subscriptions with friends. It's much cheaper than buying them at the newsagent.

* Don't use shopping as therapy. It's a very common practice, but it's very easy to overcommit yourself. Then you arrive home, still with the blues, plus an expensive purchase that doesn't really take away the pain.

* If you see some bargain film that's passed its expiry date, don't knock it back. You'll make a considerable saving on it and film can often be used quite satisfactorily for months or even years after the recommended expiry date. Keeping it in the fridge will prolong its life, too.

* Interested in saving money and having a good time while you're doing it? Invest in a copy of the magazine *Markets and Fairs*, which covers New South Wales, Victoria and Queensland. If you can't find it at your newsagent, contact Allan Rodney Wright Circulation on (02) 319 1244.

## TELEPHONE CALLS

* There's a lot of competition in the communications business these days: investigate the various cost-savings plans offered by your phone company.

* Make long-distance calls at off-peak hours for reduced costs.

* Get into the habit of putting spare change away for the phone bill, maybe the small change you clean out of your pocket or purse each day. You may wish to save the big coins but drop all the 5s, 10s and 20s into a jar. This won't save you any money on your phone bill but it won't be so painful when it comes. Or keep a money box by the phone and put cash in any time you make a call — you'd have to do it if you were using a public telephone.

* Instead of making a long-distance call, write a letter. If you have a computer, it's even easier to keep in touch this way. Write down the basic information, personalise it a little in terms of who the letter is going to, then print it off and send it. Now change those personalised details to suit another friend or family member, print that out and pop it in the mail. One basic letter does everyone but it still looks like it's been done personally. This saves time and therefore money.

## DISHWASHERS

* Do you have an economy option on your dishwasher? Use it because in most cases it will be quite adequate for the load and uses much less power.

* Cut down on power costs during a dishwasher cycle by turning off the machine before it begins drying. The dishes will be dried by the retained heat from the rinse cycle or, alternatively, open the door and let them air-dry.

* Dishwasher detergent costing you a fortune? Try substituting bicarbonate of soda or washing soda for the powder six days a week and using the normal powder on day seven. And instead of a costly rinse aid, use vinegar.

* Always read your dishwasher manual

and load the machine as the manufacturer recommends, and make sure you clean the filter regularly to prevent clogging.

* Try to run the dishwasher only when you have a full load, unless it offers several options for smaller loads.

* Connect it to the cold water supply; it will heat water for the cycle that requires hot water.

* See also the section Electrical Appliances in the chapter Heating, Cooling & Lighting.

## WHITEGOODS

* Whitegoods can be some of the most expensive household items you'll be investing in, so it's wise to shop around.

If you're in the market for a new washing machine, dishwasher or fridge, first decide what model and make you're after by browsing through an appliance store. Second, check with that store on availability, delivery, installation of the new and removal of the old. Then ring around several other stores and get their prices on the same make and model, as well as the other elements, Then make a decision on who you want to buy it from, given all the factors involved, and see if they will match the best price you've been given. You'll probably find they will.

* Also, think very carefully about the possibility of buying from a samples and seconds dealer. This doesn't mean second-hand, it means second-quality: the machine may have a scratch or a mismatched knob, which means it will be in perfectly new condition apart from that point, but has to be sold for much less than brand-new. The delivery team may well scratch your new machine when delivering it, so why not accept the mark before you buy?

* Keep your stove, dishwasher, fridge, freezer and washing machine looking as good as new — and protect them at the same time — by coating them once or twice a year with car polish. It's a particularly good idea if you're in a house that you've bought with the intention of stepping up in a few years' time. The built-in appliances will still look brand-new rather than needing a costly cosmetic or replacement job before you sell the house.

* In line with that idea, avoid using harsh abrasives to clean the top of your stove. Use foil to line the drip trays and if food does become baked on, pour on a thin layer of ammonia solution and leave for a few hours or overnight. Wipe over with plenty of hot water.

* See also the section Electrical Appliances in the chapter Heating, Cooling & Lighting.

# GREAT GIFT GIVING

Be it Christmas or birthday or anniversary or any special occasion, if you plan ahead you can save money.

## CARDS AND GIFTWRAP

- If you and/or family and friends have children, you'll always need birthday and Christmas cards and presents. So the next time you pass a bargain store with discounted greeting cards on sale, grab them. Age cards (Now you are 3, 4, 5...) will never go out of fashion.
- The same goes for giftwrap and ribbon. If it's on special, and you've got somewhere to store it, buy it. It will be a saving. I keep a drawer in the kitchen stocked with paper, ribbon and cards. If nothing else, it always has a stock of suitable-for-any-age fun birthday cards and a pile of different-coloured tissue paper and curling ribbon. I also keep scissors and sticky tape in there. If suddenly an occasion comes up, even just a quickly purchased bottle of wine to congratulate someone, the wrappings are ready.
- Why not buy your Christmas cards from a charity organisation? I think many of them are far more attractive than the glossy commercial variety, the price is often better, and having your money go where it will do something more than improve some company's bottom line is close to the real spirit of Christmas.
- Don't toss out the kindergarten 'masterpieces': they make great individual giftwraps. Consider buying some white cardboard so your child can draw or paint gift cards to match. Or have a fingerpainting session at home to specifically produce this economical giftwrap. This makes that small someone feel very special, too.

## GIFTS

- Buying in advance also makes sense for any sort of gift that's timeless and appears at a local shop on special: beautiful soaps, stationery or handkerchiefs; bargain-priced Lego starter sets; good books. If you see it and can afford it at the time, buy it then and there and put it away for the appropriate time. If it's Christmas you're planning towards, it will save on the bunfight come the middle of December.

• Remember too, there's no shame in buying the same gift for several people — chances are if one person likes it, someone else will too. And you may make an even better saving buying several when there are 'buy one and get one free' offers.

• I have several godchildren of different ages. I have made it a practice since they became interested in books to give them at least one good reference book each year, either for Christmas or their birthday. I buy these books as I see them, on special from the local bookshop or even from a book club (you can make huge savings by joining a book club). They can be atlases or dictionaries, or they can be books about space or animals or natural mysteries, whatever. I buy them and put them away until the occasion arises. The parents say the children get a great deal of pleasure from these as well as using them to look things up for school projects.

• Keep an exercise book or a computer record of your purchases. Make a list of friends and relatives you normally exchange gifts with. Draw up several columns and try to note down what you gave each other most recently so you can avoid duplication. Now work out what they might need or want this time around and make a list of those things. As you buy each gift, enter the details in your book or record.

• You might find another section in your computer record or exercise book in which you could list relevant information for gifts. For example, your best friend collects anything related to bears or frogs; she likes a certain type of perfume; her favourite colour is blue; her hobby is ... In this way you have a collection of data to draw on and you can utilise it whenever you're out shopping.

* It's a great idea to shop all through the year but it's not always something we're organised enough to do. Suddenly Christmas is here and you've got to do it all in one hit. Instead of running yourself ragged, consider buying your gifts from a catalogue. There are some excellent ones available these days and many of them are associated with charities or worthy causes, so you have a wonderful feeling of having done some good as well as solved a gift problem!

* If you've decided to give a home-grown plant as a gift, why not put it in a home-painted pot? Most craft books these days can give you instructions on how to go about it, and painting your own is a lot cheaper than buying one from a nursery or garden shop.

# HEALTH, HYGIENE AND BEAUTY

- Here is another area where bulk buying can save you money if you have storage space for the particular items.
- Consider shampoo, conditioner, soap, toilet paper and tissues but just a word of warning. Bulk soap or shampoo is not a bargain if it does disastrous things to your skin or hair. Ask if it's possible to have a trial size first; then, if you're happy, go back for the 5-litre bottle or the 144 cakes for the price of 12!
- Save on toothpaste. Simply dip your toothbrush in lemon juice and bicarbonate of soda and brush as usual. This will also make your teeth whiter. You can add a drop of peppermint oil for flavour and to freshen your breath.
- Remember to keep an eye on water usage in the bathroom. Keep your showers short; your baths not full to overflowing; and don't run the tap continuously while you're cleaning your teeth or washing your hands. And watch out for dripping taps. A tap which drips 45 drops per minute wastes about ten full bathtubs of water in a month, not to mention the added expense if it's hot water.
- To get rid of offensive odours in the toilet, use a potpourri or essential-oil burner instead of expensive air fresheners. Or simply strike a match and the smells will disappear.
- If the water in your area is hard, talk to your plumber about the cost of installing a water-softening system. It could save you a fortune in the cost of shampoo, conditioner and all household cleaning agents.
- Luxury bath treatments are a delight — no one denies that. But they can cost. Consider having a soak using bicarbonate of soda in your bath. Or use an oil such as avocado or sweet almond bought from the supermarket or health store. Add a few drops of your favourite perfume or perfumed essential oil and you've got a luxury product at a cheaper price. Or smooth the scented oil on after you've bathed and towelled dry and save yourself

the effort of cleaning the bathtub.

• Do you suffer from foot odour? Instead of constantly spending money on inner soles, cut the insole shape out of a single-layer cardboard box and replace as necessary.

• Some of the best beauty and health products you can use are very cheap and may already be tucked away in your pantry.

## HEALTHY BEAUTY

• Forget about using expensive make-up removers and skin lotions. Try petroleum jelly, baby oil or sorbolene cream. They remove make-up effectively and soften and moisturise skin at the same time. Indeed, sorbolene cream is often recommended by dermatologists for people with sensitive skin. If you do choose to buy a commercial moisturiser, look for a double-use product: a moisturiser and foundation in one, or a moisturiser with a sunscreen built in.

• Perfume will go further and last longer if you blend a drop or two with some petroleum jelly and rub this into your skin rather than spraying or dabbing the more concentrated liquid.

• Remember when you're buying beauty products that there really are only a handful of cosmetic companies, and many of them produce 'no frills' lines under other names. Think about whether you

need to buy the brand-name product. Will the expense mean a better result or is most of it in the packaging? If the packaging of the expensive product is well labelled with regard to its contents, check them against those listed for a cheaper brand. If it looks the same, go with the cheaper one.

• Investigate factory outlets or beautician supply shops, or cultivate a relationship with your hairdresser or beautician. The aim is to buy the large commercial size of the product you need, but pay the wholesale rather than the retail price.

• Think carefully, too, about whether you need to use as much of the product — any product — as the manufacturer 'recommends'. They're in business for profit, so it's in their interests for you to use as much of the product as quickly as possible so you'll buy more. Experiment with half what the instructions say: chances are it will work just as well, and your product will last twice as long. Obviously a saving.

## HAIR CARE

• When you are washing your hair, much of the shampoo can be washed away before it touches your scalp. Consider diluting your shampoo half and half with water; it will still do the job, and less is more in terms of hair health. Always pour the shampoo into your hand first, rather than directly onto the scalp; you can't see how much you're using when you tip it on directly. Not only will this save on shampoo and be healthier for your hair, but it's also healthier for the environment. Use this same approach for conditioners that you apply after the shampoo and wash out.

• Save money on conditioners that you spray on and leave on your hair by simply blending your usual conditioner with some water in a spray bottle. Proportions? Around one part conditioner to three parts water. Add more water if this blend leaves your locks too greasy; otherwise, just spray on and comb through. If you prefer to apply a leave-on conditioner by hand, towel-dry your hair after the shampoo. Then put a small amount of the conditioner on one hand and rub your hands together. Run your conditioner-dampened fingers through your hair and follow with a comb.

• Try using a good mayonnaise as a hair conditioner. Some people say it's better than the best of the real thing. Spread it on your hair, wrap your head in a warm towel, or plastic wrap, and wait 30 minutes before shampooing thoroughly.

• Using an egg white for a facial mask? (See the section For Your Face, Hands and Skin.) Use the egg yolk for a hair conditioner. Beat it until it's thick, then blend in 1 teaspoon of vegetable oil and ¼ cup of water. Shampoo first, then massage the egg mixture into your hair and leave for a few minutes before rinsing it out.

• Another good conditioner is sweet almond oil. Rub 1 or 2 tablespoons into your scalp. Then put on an old shower cap or wrap your hair with plastic wrap and leave for at least 2 hours before shampooing in the usual way.

• Troubled by dandruff? Mix ½ cup white vinegar with ½ cup of water and dab on your scalp with cottonwool balls or a soft cloth before every shampoo. Or try this remedy. Mix 2 tablespoons of vinegar with 1 tablespoon each of castor oil and bay rum. Rub the scalp thoroughly with the solution and leave on for 30 minutes before shampooing as usual. Add 2 tablespoons of vinegar to the rinsing water.

- Comb some flat beer through your hair as a setting and styling aid.

**SHAMPOO**

- Make your own shampoo from natural products, which are fully biodegradable and unlikely to irritate sensitive scalps.

- By choosing the right herbal base, you can formulate the correct mix for your hair type. For fair hair, chamomile lightens the hair (and heals scalp irritations). For dark hair, use sage or rosemary. And for oily hair, try sage, yarrow, rosemary or lime flowers.

- Combining thyme, rosemary, nettle, parsley and peppermint controls dandruff and acts as a tonic for the hair and the scalp. Prepare the herbal infusion by pouring 1 ½ litres of boiling (pure) water over 3 tablespoons of dried herbs in a ceramic bowl. Leave to steep overnight and then strain.

**HERBAL SHAMPOO**

*100 g basic soft soap (see below), grated*

*juice of 1 lemon*

*1 ½ litres of herbal infusion*

Place grated soap, lemon juice and 350 mL of the herbal infusion in a saucepan, stir and bring gently to the boil. Reduce to a simmer and stir continuously until the soap is fully dissolved. Add the remaining liquid and stir until completely combined, then cool and bottle.

## SAVING WITH SOAP

- Save money by saving soap scraps. Don't throw out the tail end of the bath soap: toss it into a jar with some water. When the jar is full of scraps, put the lot through the blender and use the mixture to fill up a liquid-soap dispenser to keep by the bathroom basin or kitchen sink. Or simply squeeze the softened scraps together, moulding them by hand or pressing them into a mould such as a muffin tray or small jelly dish.

- Another idea for soap scraps is to make some drawstring bags out of old towelling and use them to put leftover soap pieces in. Tighten and tie the drawstring and you have a ready-made washing bag.

- When you've bought soap with a slight perfume, unwrap the bars and use them to scent your underwear, scarves and the like. When it comes time to use them as soap, these bars will have dried out in the air and will last longer — and your clothes will smell fresh too!

## SOAP MAKING

**FOR ALL CLEANSING**

- You can make your own soap of different kinds for all purposes.

- Tallow makes the hardest soap but bacon fat, sausage grease and dripping work well too. Or you can use clean white lard, which you can buy cheaply from most supermarkets. Vegetable shortening or tallow can also be used. All vegetable oils work well in combination with each other or with fats; in fact, a fat and oil combination makes the best toilet soap.

- The best water to use is rainwater. Or buy a cask of purified water at the supermarket. Hard water can be softened by adding some washing soda or borax. A side benefit of this treatment is that the resulting soap is creamy and lathers well.
- You will need a large glass or ceramic mixing bowl and a large enamel saucepan. Do not use any bowls or utensils made of aluminium, iron, tin or plastic as the caustic soda will eat them away.
- You will also need a wooden spoon; moulds for the soap (cake pans or milk cartons, or fancy chocolate or cooking moulds lined with damp calico); rubber gloves for handling the caustic soda; and a large knife to cut the soap into bars. Keep all utensils only for soap making.
- If you are recycling your cooking oil, strain it first. You will also need to purify your fat or dripping. To remove salt, place the fat in the saucepan and cover with water. Bring to the boil, then remove from the heat and allow to cool. Boiling the fat in water allows salt and other impurities to sink to the bottom of the saucepan.
- Now skim the fat off and clarify. To do this, heat it gently to melting point in the enamel saucepan. Skim off any pieces of meat and then strain through muslin or through a fat strainer, available from major supermarkets or kitchen shops.
- Some basic rules about soap making are always to add the caustic soda to water; add the caustic mixture to the fat/oil in a slow stream; pour the mixture into moulds once it has cooled and developed a texture like honey; and store the soap in a stack which allows air circulation while it's curing (all soap should be cured for several weeks so it hardens properly and lasts longer).

## CREAMY WHITE SOAP

*350 g caustic soda*
*750 mL olive oil*
*1 L water*
*2 kg tallow*

Put the water in the ceramic bowl and add the caustic soda carefully, stirring until it's dissolved. The mix becomes very hot and must rest until it cools to lukewarm before completing the recipe.

Melt the tallow gently and allow to cool but not to re-solidify. Add the oil. Gently add the caustic solution to the tallow and oil and stir for 5 minutes. Pour into moulds and cut into bars (if desired) as soon as the soap sets, or else it will crumble. Cure for at least two or three weeks before using.

## BASIC SOFT SOAP

*500 g caustic soda*
*1 ½ L pure soft water*
*1 ½ L vegetable or seed oil*

Put the water in the ceramic bowl and add the caustic soda carefully, stirring until it's dissolved. The mix becomes very hot and must rest until it cools to lukewarm before completing the recipe.

Carefully add the caustic mix to the oil (unheated) and stir for 5 minutes. Pour into moulds and store in a warm spot for around 24 hours before cutting into bars and allowing to cure for several weeks.

## HEBAL SOAP AND SCENTED SOAP

- You will no doubt experiment with different combinations, but here are two suggestions for improving your basic soap.
- To make herbal soap, soak your herbs overnight in the water you're going to use. Choose your specific herb and use 2 teaspoons of dried leaves or flowers (or 8 tablespoons of fresh) for every 600 mL

of water. Bring the water to boiling point and pour over the herbs in a ceramic bowl. Cover and leave overnight, then strain in the morning. (Check with a good herbal book or a health shop for the healing properties of various herbs.)

• To scent the soap, add a few drops of the appropriate essential flower or herb oils just before you pour the soap mix into the moulds.

## FOR FRESHENING THE AIR

• Make your own herbal air freshener. Choose a disinfectant herb from this list: thyme, orange flower, bergamot, juniper, clove, lavender, peppermint, rosemary, sandalwood, eucalyptus. Use its essential oil to make your freshener.

*24–30 drops essential oil*

*5 mL vodka*

*500 mL distilled water (such as the ironing aid 'Clean Steam', at supermarkets)*

Dissolve the essential oil in the vodka and add to the distilled water.

Store in a pump-spray bottle. Shake well to mix and use with the fine mist setting.

You can also make the freshener with dried herbs.

*6 to 8 teaspoons dried herbs*

*10 mL vodka*

*500 mL distilled water*

Put the herbs in an enamel saucepan, add the water and bring to the boil. Simmer for 5 minutes. Remove from the stove and cover, allowing it to steep overnight. Strain through muslin cloth or stocking, squeezing all liquid from the herbs. Stir in the vodka until well blended.

• Make your own pomander. Cover a ripe thin-skinned orange with cloves until completely covered. Roll in two teaspoons of orris root (from a health food store) and two teaspoons of cinnamon mixed together. Wrap the orange in a tissue and store in a dark cupboard until it has hardened. It will need tobe left for up to eight weeks. Press a staple into the top of the orange and tie a bow on, or thread a ribbon through and then hang from the clothes rail in your cupboard. They keep clothes smelling sweet, and keep moths away, and they're more pleasant, and cheaper, than commercial pest repellants.

## FOR YOUR FACE, HANDS AND SKIN

• Soak a small amount of bran and/or oatmeal in water or milk and mash to a paste. Now massage your skin with a little oil (try combining olive with vegetable oil, or use avocado or sweet almond oil). Pat on the oatmeal paste and leave for several minutes before sponging away with a face washer wrung out in warm water.

• Boil a few tablespoons of your favourite dried herbs in a saucepan of water for a few minutes. Take the pan off the heat, lean over it and make a tent over your head and the pan with a towel. Allow the steam to work on your skin for about 5 minutes, then rinse your face, and splash with cold water to close the pores.

• Peel a section of cucumber and rub the inside of the peel over your skin and leave the juice to dry. This astringent is particularly refreshing in hot weather. Cucumber slices also ease tired eyes.

• Make a facial mask by whipping the white of an egg till it's getting stiff and

then patting it over your face. Allow it to dry and tighten, then rinse off with a face washer wrung out in warm water.

• Make your own hand cleaners. Combine equal parts of glycerine, lemon juice and methylated spirits; or fine oatmeal mixed with a little lemon juice; or a little bit of white fat and a teaspoon of sugar. Rub it in well, then wash as usual with soap and warm water.

• Make a herbal hand cleaner that will remove ingrained dirt and stains from your hands — and is gentle on them, too.

> 30 mL olive oil
> 20 mL avocado oil
> sugar
> ½ teaspoon dried sage
> ½ teaspoon dried yarrow

Finely grind the herbs and mix them together. Add them to the combined oils with enough sugar to form a paste. Keep in a screw-top jar and rub over your hands when necessary.

• Make your own hand lotion by mixing 1 dessertspoon each of lemon juice, honey, olive oil and glycerine. Keep in a bottle and shake well before use.

• Make your own bath oil. A simple version is to blend 30 drops of your favourite herb or flower essential oil with 40 mL of almond oil (from health food stores or some supermarkets). Store in a dark glass bottle. Add 10 drops of the mixture to the bath while the taps are running.

• Try a combination of essential oils. Use

2 drops each of rosemary, bay leaf, and pennyroyal and 4 drops of lime flower for a calming and relaxing bath. Use 5 drops of hyssop, 3 of rosemary and 2 of bay leaf in your bath to ease tired muscles.

- Make your own shaving cream. Combine one small packet of Lux Flakes with 300 mL boiling water and beat together until dissolved. Add 1 dessertspoon of olive oil and a few drops of your preferred essential oil or perfume. Beat again until thick and creamy. Keep in screw-top jars or plastic bottles.

## FOR YOUR HEALTH

### MAKING YOUR OWN LINIMENT

*1 cup vinegar*

*1 cup turpentine*

*1 beaten egg*

*1 cake camphor, grated*

*1 teaspoon double-distilled eucalyptus oil*

*2 tablespoons olive oil*

Put all ingredients into a large bottle and shake well. This liniment improves with age and will keep for years.

### MAKING YOUR OWN VAPOUR RUB

- For Version 1, place 115 g of petroleum jelly in a soup bowl and grate into it 2 cakes of natural (not synthetic) camphor. Add 3 teaspoonsful of double-distilled eucalyptus oil and mix thoroughly before pouring into jars. Stand the jars in hot water on the stove to allow the mix to settle. Keep the mixture airtight.

- For Version 2, mix 2 tablespoons of methylated spirits with 4 tablespoons of olive oil and 4 cakes of natural (not synthetic) camphor. Melt the mix over a slow heat until it boils and thickens, then bottle.

### MAKING YOUR OWN COUGH MIXTURE

- For Version 1, mix together equal quantities of honey, lemon juice and malt vinegar. Sip 1 tablespoon of the mixture when the cough is bad. More can be taken when necessary.

- For Version 2, boil 125 g washed whole garlic in 3 cups of water until liquid is reduced by half. Strain and add 1 cup each of honey and malt or cider vinegar. Simmer for 5 minutes, then cool and bottle. If you have some lemons available, add the juice of 2 lemons to the brew.

- For Version 3, mix 250 g of honey, 4 tablespoons of glycerine, 3 tablespoons of olive oil and the juice of 3 lemons in a saucepan and bring slowly to the boil. Allow to cool, then bottle.

### MAKING YOUR OWN COUGH DROPS

Boil together for 8 minutes 3 tablespoons each of sugar and honey, and 1 tablespoon each of butter, vinegar and lemon juice. Test to see if it's ready by dropping a little into cold water: it's ready if it's brittle. Stir in 15 drops double-distilled eucalyptus oil and pour into a shallow greased tray. When cold, break into small pieces and store in a jar in the fridge.

# BORROWING AND BUDGETING

* Shopping for money is no different from shopping for any other commodity — it pays to look around and check out all that's on offer. Talk to your bank, and your bank's opposition; talk to credit unions and building societies. Compare not only the interest rate but all the little extras like terms, establishment fees and flexibility on repayments, and then work out what works best for you. If you really want to stick with your present financial institution but they haven't offered the best deal, go back to them with the information you have and see if they can match it. Lending money is big business and highly competitive. Everyone in that business needs customers, so make the system work in your favour.

* If you're thinking about buying something fairly costly, talk to your bank manager about a loan for the purchase, rather than putting it on your credit card. The interest charges will be lower.

* Start a savings plan. You can put away a lot of money quite quickly if you do it in small but regular amounts. Decide on a sum you can realistically afford, even if it's only $10 a week, then stick to it. It will add up faster than you think. Consider opening a special account for your savings, perhaps at an institution where you don't normally do business, so you won't be tempted to dip into it. An added bonus is you establish a savings record with a second financial institution, which could be a useful alternative when it comes time to borrow the big dollars.

* Get into the habit of clearing your pockets and wallet of loose change every night, and putting it into a piggy bank that you have to destroy to reach the money: you'll think twice about doing so.

* Consider keeping certain coins out for specific purposes such as parking meters and bridge tolls and keep them in a special purse in the car.

## BUYING A HOME

• Buying a home is probably the biggest purchase you'll ever make, and the biggest sum you'll ever borrow. Your mortgage term could be 10, 15, 20 years or more, but that doesn't have to be set in concrete. Instead of paying the prescribed payment obediently from month to month and year to year, investigate what happens if you budget to pay just a little more, or to make your payments fortnightly rather than monthly. The savings can be huge. Talk to your bank manager or financial adviser about a system that will work for you without putting pressure on your pocket.

• Other ways of knocking the mortgage down to size include raising the payments in line with yearly salary increases and pumping windfalls such as your winnings from the office Melbourne Cup sweep, or a few dollars from a Lotto payout, directly into the mortgage. It all builds up and you can decrease the length of the loan as well as save on interest charges: your home might be yours within 10 years instead of 20.

## SETTING A BUDGET

• First, make an honest assessment of your financial position. Work out what your annual income is, and what your annual outgoings are. These will include the bills or costs that come up once a year, which we'll call periodic expenses, and the ones that crop up every day, week or month, which are frequent expenses. The aim of the exercise is not only to cover these costs, but to have money left over for a savings plan. If expenses outweigh income, you have some serious work to do.

• The largest periodic expenses include council and water rates, insurance and regular house maintenance (mortgage or rent payments come under the category of frequent expenses). With rates, pay quarterly if that option is available and if you're able to remember, or work out a regular amount to take from your pay packet to cover them, and bank it in an account with a higher interest rate, drawing it out for the one-off payment when it's due.

• An insurance bill is often a shock when it arrives, but the alternative could be much worse: very few of us could find a spare $50,000 to replace the contents of our home, should it be burned out, let alone the replacement cost of the house itself. Again, work out what all your insurance

(health, life, accident, house, contents, car) costs and put that money aside regularly from your pay packet.

- There are always little extras that need doing to the house each year, and timber homes need more maintenance than brick ones. Here, too, the best idea could be to set an amount and bank it regularly. Talk to your bank manager about the advisability of an account which holds the mortgage payment plus regular deposits to cover the big bills. You might choose at the end of each year, if there hasn't been a major expense, to use some of that extra to pay off a little more of the mortgage.

- Other periodic expenses which might be budgeted for regularly are the cost of replacing a major household item, such as a fridge or washing machine, and the power, gas and phone bills. Then that money will be gathering interest until it's required. (Another possibility with the phone is keeping a money box nearby and paying as you make each call.)

- Other major periodic expenses to consider may be school fees, medical costs, holidays, car expenses (rego, insurance, tyres, maintenance), the cost of belonging to social and sporting clubs, Christmas gifts and major charity donations.

- Frequent expenses include mortgage, rent or board costs, food (this is where you can cut down by making your garden work for you), cigarettes and alcohol, clothes and grooming, public transport, credit card repayments, entertainment, newspapers and magazines, and if you occasionally have a flutter on the horses or Lotto, gambling.

- After the two columns are drawn up, if it looks like spending will exceed income, you'll have to look at ways of finding more money, if that's possible, and ways to cut back on your outgoings. Some things like rates and insurance are impossible to cut, so have a look at other areas. Maybe your lifestyle will have to be a little less lavish.

- Planning carefully in the short term will pay long-term benefits. And it won't take long before you get into the swing of things and know exactly what's coming up and when. Perhaps in the meantime, it may be worth keeping a calendar which specifically reminds you of when bills are due to arrive and the approximate cost of each.

# OFFICE SAVINGS

Money-saving ideas seem to be just the ticket for ourselves and our families, but we can do a lot at work too, which is good news for the boss and may well pay dividends for you (does the company have a prize for clever suggestions?) and the environment.

## PAPER

• Get into the habit of recycling paper. Don't throw paper away that's only been used on one side when you're finished with it, or a piece of paper that you typed and made a mistake on. Use the other side of the sheet for photocopying, or staple several sheets together to make notepads ready for quick scribbles. Add another out-tray to each desk so people get into the habit of putting paper with only one use into it, ready for using again. Install two bins in the office: one for paper and one for garbage. Make sure your company is involved in recycling paper it can't use rather than tossing it in the bin — someone can benefit. Arrange to have it collected.

• Save paper in other ways. Talk to a colleague rather than writing a memo; put up a bulletin board and encourage people to check it daily and use it instead of sending a memo to everyone; install a loudspeaker system so announcements can be made rather than written and sent around. And if you are installing a bulletin board, consider using a whiteboard or a blackboard which can be written on, rather than one that pieces of paper are pinned on.

• If the office usually shreds old documents and then pays to have the shredded paper carted away, talk to your local zoo. Zoos can use shredded paper as bedding for their apes and monkeys, and, often, the soiled paper is removed each day and used as compost for the zoo gardens. If you work in the Sydney area, the Taronga Zoo will probably be able to arrange a regular collection from your office. Any surplus of their soiled paper goes to the Royal Botanic Gardens.

• Reuse envelopes wherever possible. Write a new address on a label or piece of paper and stick it over the old one. Obviously not the tactic to use with a new client, but for general daily messages, getting a second use out of a perfectly

**THE ULTIMATE BOOK OF MONEY HINTS**

good envelope makes more sense than tossing it in the bin, and is going to save money in the long run. If you have regular clients with envelopes constantly going between offices by courier, why not suggest an interoffice-type envelope system with several address spaces on the front. How often does a large expensive manila envelope get used only once?

## AROUND THE OFFICE

• Bring your own mug to the office instead of using polystyrene cups for coffee and tea. Consider bringing a glass for your spring water or buy a set of glasses for the office for the spring-water supply.

• Turn off lights when you don't need them. Do the lights in the toilet need to be on all day or just when someone is in there? Are there ways to improve the lighting in your area with more efficient bulbs or tubes? Are there any other power users which could be switched off between uses, such as tools or machines?

• Don't recycle just paper, either. Consider installing two bins in the kitchen area, one for glass and one for cans. Educate people to put their lunchtime bottles and cans in the appropriate spot, and then educate the cleaners to put them out for pick-up, or arrange to do it yourselves within the office team. If you collect enough cans, the money you get back from recycling them could go in the social club kitty!

* Consider using refillable pens and pencils, rather than tossing away empty pens and pencil stubs.

* Consider using fabric hand towels rather than paper ones in the bathroom, and use tea towels in the tea room. If you're in a small office, make a roster for washing them.

* Put a jug in the tea room for boiling water instead of using an urn or an instant hot water heater. Then people are only boiling what they need. Make sure it's an automatic cut-off model so it doesn't boil dry.

* Does your company make anything that leaves what could be a useful by-product? Or do you regularly receive large posting cylinders, boxes or other items that you can't use or easily recycle? Instead of paying a garbage contractor to remove them, check with the zoo or with schools, kindergartens or the local reverse garbage centre in your area. These organisations are often on the lookout for other people's cast-off material, either for entertaining their primate collection or for creative use by children, and they may be happy to collect it from you. As a little twist on the old adage that one man's meat is another man's poison, consider that one office's garbage could be a creative person's raw material. Find out if you can become a regular source of such material, and keep the office clean while saving money.

## EQUIPMENT

* Ask the powers that be to invest in covers and other protective gear for the computer system. Computers are expensive to buy and there's little return on second-hand equipment. Protect them by covering them every night and think about other ways of protecting them, such as no drinking or eating or smoking near them. It's a long-term saving.

* Investigate whether your printer will take a refillable toner cartridge instead of using one-use cartridges.

## REFURNISHING

And when it comes time to refurnish the office, does it all need to be new? Given how quickly technology changes, many items are superseded as soon as they leave the showroom. Talk to the boss about whether a reconditioned or superseded model of a fax, photocopier or printer would do the job. Do you really need 'new' furniture such as chairs, desks and filing cabinets? There are plenty of companies that specialise in second-hand office furniture and fittings and they may have just what you need at a fraction of the price it would be if new. For a small business, or for those just starting out working for themselves, good-quality second-hand equipment makes a lot of sense.

# PENNYWISE PEST CONTROL

- If you have been bitten by an insect, use raw onion juice to relieve the itch. Or try a dab of methylated spirits or eucalyptus oil, or a combination of equal quantities of cold tea and methylated spirits. Honey is an antidote for a bee sting.
- You can keep pests away easily by using everyday products rather than expensive and perhaps toxic pesticides.

## ANTS

- Keep ants out of the garden with this mix which is not dangerous to children or plants: dissolve 250 g salt in 2 cups of water, then mix in 5 kg of sawdust or bran and about 10 cups of molasses. It's a very crumbly mixture which you spread around plants and shrubs.
- Keep them away from the sink by cutting a lemon in half and rubbing along their pathway.
- Sprinkle black pepper under rugs to deter them (and silverfish).
- Sprinkle ant tracks with powdered borax or talcum powder.
- Combine 2 cups of sugar, 1 cup of water and 2 tablespoons each of borax and boric acid and boil for 3 minutes. Put a few drops in saucers or the lids of jars and place in the path of the ants. Dispose of when full.
- Sprinkle sugar where ants can get at it and then follow them to their nest. Pour turpentine, kerosene or paraffin into the nest.
- Sprinkle crushed cloves near the nest to deter ants and put whole cloves near the point of entry and around cupboards and the kitchen sink.

## APHIDS

- Mix 1 tablespoon of Epsom salts and 1 teaspoon of Condy's crystals in a bucket of water and spray around affected plants once a fortnight.

**THE ULTIMATE BOOK OF MONEY HINTS**

- Grow garlic under roses or other plants affected by aphids or boil some onions in water and, when cold, sprinkle the strained water around the plants.

## BLOWFLIES

- Flies hate basil, so grow it in pots and keep them near doorways. Not only will this keep the flies away, but the basil is a great addition to summer foods, especially tomatoes.

## BORERS

- Spray kerosene or cloudy ammonia into their holes to kill them. Don't refill holes with woodfiller unless you are certain all the borers are dead. It's worth calling in a professional if you suspect further activity.

## COCKROACHES

- Sprinkle their pathways liberally with highly perfumed talcum powder.

- Buy a vanilla pod from a health food store and put pieces around areas normally frequented by cockroaches. They hate the smell.
- Mix 4 tablespoons of borax with 2 tablespoons of plain flour or sugar and 1 tablespoon of cocoa. Leave in saucers or upturned lids in areas where cockroaches scuttle. Be sure children and pets can't get at this as borax is poisonous.
- Use empty but unwashed margarine or butter containers for this method. Pour in about 1 cm of wine or beer or put in a slice of banana. Leave overnight in areas cockroaches frequent: they will climb into the container to get at the sweet substance but won't be able to climb out again because of the greasy walls.
- Sprinkle Epsom salts in cupboards and any area that cockroaches frequent. Replenish every few weeks to keep them at bay.

## CRICKETS

Do you have crickets in the roof? Buy 25 g carbaryl from a plant nursery and mix it with 1 kg of bran and ¼ cup of powdered milk in a plastic bag. Seal the bag and set aside for 24 hours, then place the mixture in small piles in the roof.

## EARWIGS

Collect about a dozen empty tins and smear the insides with a liberal dose of fishpaste. Now up-end them on garden stakes around your plants. The next day, half-fill a bucket with hot water and add a generous slurp of kerosene. Hold the bucket under each tin and tap the tin to release the pests. Bury the lot in a hole in the garden.

## FLEAS

- When washing the dog, add a tablespoon of salt to the water to help kill fleas.
- Spray mineral turpentine from a pump-spray bottle onto the back of carpets and rugs.
- Fleas hate mint so put some fresh mint under mattresses and mats and change frequently.
- Dissolve 3 natural camphor blocks in about 2 cups of methylated spirits and rub onto carpet or mattress. Fleas don't like the smell.
- Pick a bunch of mint, chop it finely and pour a couple of litres of boiling water over it. Stir well and allow to stand for 15 minutes. Sweep it over the carpet. The fleas will soon surface. Be ready for them and kill them by wiping over the carpet surface with a cloth wrung out in kerosene.

## FLIES

- Put a piece of sponge rubber on an old saucer and moisten the rubber with 1 teaspoon of oil of lavender and 2 tablespoons of boiling water. Add a little hot water each day and top up the oil with an extra drop or two twice a week.
- Wipe over doorframes and window frames with oil of lavender, raw onion juice, kerosene or vinegar. Wipe windows and mirrors with kerosene or vinegar, too, and then polish with a dry cloth.
- Plant herbs such as pennyroyal,

wormwood, tansy, fennel and basil in pots or near the back door or window. Mint is also a great insect repellent as it deters ants, aphids, cabbage butterfly, caterpillars, fleas, beetles and moths as well as flies.

• Place a hanging basket or pot of ferns near the door or window where flies most often come in.

• Tie a few whole cloves in a small piece of muslin and hang on light fittings where flies congregate.

• If you have horses, plant a walnut tree to repel stable flies.

## FRUIT FLY

Make a bait for these pests by taking an ice-cream container and cutting two holes in the sides just over halfway up. Each hole should be about 25 mm in diameter. Then make four or five small holes in the top, each about 5 mm in diameter. The bait is made from a mix of 300 g of pulped orange, 15 g of ammonium carbonate (from chemists) and 600 mL of cold water. Store in a tightly lidded (and labelled, POISON!) bottle in the fridge until it is needed. To bait the trap, put in 10 mL of the mixture and add another 300 mL of cold water, then put the lid on and hang the trap in a string harness in a shady part of the tree. Empty and recharge about once a week. To make the trap even more efficient, add 1 drop of detergent to 2 L of water and then use 300 mL of this mix instead of plain cold water. It reduces the surface tension of the water to make sure the flies drown.

## LICE

- Fresh air, sunshine and disinfectant are the remedies you need. If the lice are in clothing, rinse the clothing in a disinfectant. Turn the clothing inside out and dry outside so that the air and sun can reach the seams and kill any nits (eggs) that may be hidden there.
- A hot iron rubbed over clothes (especially seams) will kill nits, as will putting the clothes into the tumble drier for about 20 minutes.
- Use a special shampoo for treating lice or wash hair with vinegar and water and comb through with a fine lice comb.
- Comb through hair daily with drops of either pure essential oil of thyme or tincture of thyme (from specialist herb or health food stores) until the problem clears. It's a powerful antiseptic.

## MICE

- Sprinkle around cupboards and under the oven and sink with oil of peppermint, oil of cloves or cayenne pepper to suggest they should go elsewhere.
- Plug the mouse hole with steel wool. They can't chew through it.
- Sprinkle naphthalene flakes around skirting boards, under lounge cushions and in cupboards.
- Mice detest the smell of mint so leave sprigs anywhere they like to frequent.
- Mix together equal parts of dry cement (or plaster of Paris) and flour (or cornflour) and place in saucers or upturned lids near areas where mice and rats hang out. They eat the mixture, go away to find water which mixes with the powder and they end up very dead. This is a cheap and highly effective alternative to rodent poison.

## MITES

- Fresh sprigs of mint under the carpet and in the cupboards will help get rid of an onslaught of mites. If they're in the bed linen, wash it in wool mix and dry outside in the fresh air.
- Mites like warmth so try to fit the affected items in the fridge. For example, put one pillow at a time in a plastic bag and leave for at least an hour in the fridge.

## MOSQUITOS

- A few drops of spirits of camphor (from chemists) on a lump of sugar placed on the bedside table will keep mosquitos away at night.
- Burn citronella or lavender oil (or lavender incense) in an essential-oil burner, or buy a special citronella or eucalyptus candle for outdoor entertaining.

- A pot of basil on the windowsill outside the bedroom will deter mozzies.
- Plant old-fashioned castor-oil plants in the garden to keep mosquitos at bay. Plant them close to doors, windows and entertaining areas but not too close as they can grow to be anywhere from two to eight metres in height.
- Save prunings from herb plants, especially lavender, and toss them on the barbecue fire. Pennyroyal will also work, as will green eucalyptus leaves, but they make the fire very smoky.

## MOTHS

- They hate coming anywhere near cupboard drawers which have been wiped over with a strong ammonia solution.
- They also hate cloves. Keep wardrobes and drawers moth-free and smelling fresh by buying a supply of whole cloves in tins. Pierce the tins several times to allow the aroma to circulate and then leave the tins in areas where you keep clothes or foodstuffs that moths like.
- Sprinkle Epsom salts in corners of cupboards, wardrobes and under carpets.
- Sprinkle oil of cinnamon on cotton wool balls and place these among your clothes.
- Use a pomander to keep them at bay. Stick whole cloves in a ripe thin-skinned orange, starting at the stalk end, until the orange is completely covered. Roll it in 2 teaspoons of orris root (from a health food store) and 2 teaspoons of cinnamon mixed together. Wrap the orange in a

tissue and store in a dark cupboard until it has hardened. It will need to be left for up to eight weeks. Press a staple into the top of the orange and tie on a bow, or thread a ribbon through and then hang the pomander from the clothes rail in your cupboard. It will last for about three years, keeping moths at bay and giving a gentle perfume to clothing.

• Dried sage is another herb moths and other indoor insects are not partial to: sprinkle it in the linen or kitchen cupboards.

## POSSUMS

• They can seem like a pest but we live in one of the few countries in the world lucky enough still to have native wildlife living near our cities.

• Instead of trying to exterminate the animal, call your local council, the zoo or a group such as the Wildlife Information and Rescue Service (WIRES) to trap and relocate the possum. WIRES actually encourages you to keep the possum, but in the garden rather than the roof, and can help with providing a possum box as an alternative nest.

## SANDFLIES

• Stop the itch of bites by dabbing with Vicks VapoRub, equal quantities of cold tea and methylated spirits or a mix of equal parts of Dettol, olive oil and methylated spirits. This will also help keep them at bay.

• Smear olive oil lightly around the eyes to keep the pests away.

• Dab some citronella on the skin.

## SILVERFISH

• Regularly vacuum books, bookshelves and boxes where books are stored to stop silverfish infestations settling in.

• Place bunches of dried lavender, or a mix of lavender and bay leaves, in storage boxes; wipe over shelves with lavender oil; and scatter dried lavender and bay leaves among the books when you put them back.

• Sprinkle black pepper under rugs to deter them (and ants).

• Encourage a friendly spider such as a huntsman to move into the library because they eat silverfish and other pests.

## SLUGS

• Heat some cabbage leaves in the oven or microwave until soft. Then coat the leaves with unsalted butter or clean dripping. Put the leaves in the garden and once they are covered with slugs, destroy them.

## SNAILS

• Mix together equal quantities of lime, soot and bran and sprinkle around the edges of garden beds.

• Sprinkle sawdust around plants that you don't want eaten: snails won't cross the sawdust.

**SNAIL SPRAY 1**
Soak 100 g chopped garlic in 2 tablespoons of liquid paraffin for 48 hours, then add ½ litre of water and 30 g pure soap. Filter the mixture and store in a plastic container. When you

want to use it, add 3 teaspoons of the mix to 1 litre of water and use in a pump-spray bottle. This solution also works on other pests, especially small sucking insects and soft-bodied larvae.

**SNAIL SPRAY 2**

Chop up a whole bulb of garlic (not 1 clove) and soak for four days in 2 teaspoons of liquid paraffin. Mix up 20 g oil-based soap with 1 litre of water and strain before adding it to the garlic pulp, mixing at the ratio of 1 part garlic to 99 parts water. The mixture gains in strength and efficacy the longer you let it stand. Store in airtight jars and spray, using a pump-spray bottle.

## TERMITES

• Don't mess around if you suspect termites: these guys can cost big dollars, so call in a professional. But to help minimise the risk: keep rubbish and woodpiles away from the outside walls of your house; inspect sheds, garages and under the house every six months for signs of activity; and don't store loose timber or wooden boxes under the house. Dampness, timber and termites are a lethal combination, so make sure they don't mix. Once you've had one professional inspection, keep it up.

• Always have a pest inspection before buying a new house.

## WEEVILS

• Tape a few bay leaves under the lids of the flour and sugar canisters to deter weevils.

• For dried fruit, add a slice of lemon rind to the storage jar.

• Sprinkle salt around the shelves where food is stored.

• Hang small cloth sacks of black pepper in food storage cupboards.

• Wipe over cupboard shelf surfaces with lavender oil to deter moths.

# RECYCLING

- Supermarket carrier bags make excellent garbage bin liners, and it's so easy to tie the handles over the top of a full bag. Maybe you can move the old big bin outside for recycling bottles and invest in a smaller bin for inside which the supermarket bags fit perfectly.

- And how about a benchtop tidy with a plastic bag from a bread loaf as a liner? Make sure there are no holes in it, or use several, one on top of another, then scrape dirty dinner plates into this bin to save splashing mess over the other one.

- Or, instead, do yourself and the environment a favour. Use your laundry basket for shopping. Refuse the plastic

bags, keep your groceries in the supermarket trolley and push it to the car. You can then load your groceries directly into the basket. At home, use your laundry basket trolley to wheel your shopping inside. Result? No broken bags or broken grocery items, no heavy lifting, and no new pile of plastic bags that you can't find a use for.

• Old roll-on deodorant bottles with easily removable balls make an ideal paint pen for the small fry. Remove the ball and fill with nontoxic paint; replace the ball and lid until needed for a different painting experience. They also make handy containers for sunscreen; it's easier to apply the lotion than wiping it on by hand.

• Old plastic ice-cream containers, margarine tubs and takeaway food containers have myriad uses. Cut them into oblong strips with pointed ends and write on them for plant markers; leave them whole for lunch boxes; cut a small hole in the bottom of one, then place knitting wool inside and replace the lid. This stops the wool tangling and getting dirty as you knit or crochet. You can use them as storage for playdough, puzzles, pencils and crayons; for freezing the other half of the double-quantity casserole you've prepared (smaller containers make ideal one-serve-size freezer containers for busy families on different schedules); for seed propagation (put holes in the lid); for fishing tackle boxes or for storing shoe-cleaning materials.

• Old yogurt containers are great for growing individual seedlings or as paint pots for the little ones.

• Old milk cartons are useful in lots of ways. You can three-quarter fill them with water and freeze for use as picnic ice bricks. Or use them as planter boxes for seedlings: perforate the bottom before you fill them with soil so it is easy to remove at transplanting time. When you're painting the house, use them to hold a small amount of paint for a touch-up job, or soak your brushes in them.

• Check with your local kindergarten or reverse garbage centre. They may be able to use old egg cartons, toilet roll or plastic wrap cylinders, fabric, Christmas and birthday cards and wrapping paper.

• To recycle household goods that have done you good service but aren't really part of the current plan, consider having a garage sale. Your local council may have regulations regarding them, so check with them first. Commonsense should prevail: make sure everything has a price and be realistic about it. After all, the alternative is throwing it away. If possible, stack the goods outside (or, indeed, in the garage!); have plenty of change and a supply of carry bags; and be prepared for an early start. People will inevitably turn up much earlier than the time you've advertised in the paper, on the local bulletin board or on nearby power poles.

• Or, instead of holding a garage sale, investigate local council rulings on markets in the area and/or car boot sales. Gather your goodies together and be part of one of them. You'll probably attract a wider audience than you would to a garage sale and it possibly makes more sense from a security point of view since people are not visiting your home. Also you won't have people arriving on your doorstep at ungodly hours, nor will you lose a whole day if you don't need that much time to sell what you have.

• Local councils do much these days in terms of recycling, but for lesser known objects and materials, speak to your state pollution control centre for details of what

recycling services are available for things like tyres, car batteries, oil and the like.

• Never wash cooking oil down the drain. Pour it into an empty can or bottle and seal it before putting it in the garbage, or recycle it for another cooking session or for homemade soap. Or buy a special container now at supermarkets that absorbs old oil. It can also be used as fuel for the barbecue. The ultimate cost of pouring oil down the sink is increased water pollution and increased water rates as the relevant authorities battle to clean up our waterways.

• Never wash any form of poison container out under running water. If it's glass it should not be recycled but disposed of as garbage; simply seal tightly and put out for rubbish collection or for a special toxic chemicals collection. Again, the immediate cost is not evident but the ultimate cost is the price of restoring our waterways to the way they should be.

• Don't toss out old or odd woollen socks. They make excellent polishing cloths: just slip one on each hand.

• Save old jars for homemade jam or marmalade, and recycle them time and time again. The particularly stylish ones, such as some coffee jars, could be used for jam or homemade sauce that you plan to give to friends.

- Save old pump-spray bottles from commercial cleaners. Clean them out thoroughly and use them for your homemade garden and pest sprays.

# RENOVATING

## BATHROOMS

- If you're doing up the bathroom, consider buying seconds in tiles, particularly if you're using a plain colour. You'd be hard-pressed to pick the difference, and you can spend a little extra on first-quality border tiles to add a touch of class.
- Do you need to renovate the bathroom, but again are short on funds? In the meantime, make it look larger by installing the largest mirror that will fit and that you can afford. It will change the look of the room.
- When you're renovating a bathroom, consider going plain white and then highlighting with plants, towels and other knick-knacks. Plain white tiles and fittings are cheaper than coloured, and give you much more scope when you get tired of the trim colour you've been using. It also makes the house more saleable. Bathrooms can be expensive renovations and if a potential buyer doesn't like your choice, it could mean no sale.

## WALLS AND FLOORS

- Would you like wallpaper but don't think you can afford it? How about painting some stripes on the walls? Simply use masking tape to define your lines and paint away. Start with your base colour. Then when it's dry, use masking tape to mark the sides of the stripes and paint the desired contrast colour between the masking-tape defining lines. Peel off when dry. Simple but smart.
- Use the same technique for a new-look floor. If you're stuck with a plain masonite or concrete base waiting for carpet, why not paint some tiles, or marble? Again, mark out the sections with masking tape or a piece of string tied between two nails, and paint away. You're only limited by your imagination. For tiles, start with a plain base coat and put in the contrasts, followed by a layer or two of clear Estapol; for marble effects, check with a book on painted finishes. Either way you'll end up with a reasonably cheap floor finish that you may decide is too good to replace with anything else.
- Do the walls of the bedroom need replastering or wallpapering and right now you don't have the money? Buy some cheap calico or some other easy-to-drape fabric and staple-gun or glue it to the walls, á la sheikh's tent, for a romantic look in the meantime.
- You can use calico or something similar if you're in need of a window trim but can't yet afford full curtains, or if you simply want to frame a window rather than cover it. Drape the fabric over the curtain rod and let it hang casually.

- If you have walls that need replastering but you don't want to do it just yet for lack of funds, consider using a bold wallpaper that will camouflage the imperfections.
- If plaster really does need replacing, consider the option of timber panelling instead. If the room will take it, it's a far less messy and therefore, depending on the room size, far less costly option.

## KITCHENS

- Looking for a cheap decoration for the kitchen? Consider a collection of mundane kitchen bits-and-pieces: either mount them on the wall on their own, or turn them into a work of art, mounted on a piece of board and framed in old fence palings.
- No money for a new kitchen table and chairs after you've done the renovations? Search the local second-hand stores, or even St Vincent's or Salvation Army op-shops. Odd chairs are not a problem if they're similar in colour or finish and providing they surround an interesting table. Link them with matching seat cushions.
- Redoing the kitchen floor? Order a few extra tiles and halve them for a new splashback on the benchtop. Replace the old kitchen benchtops in colour-coordinated laminex, which is a reasonable alternative to a full renovation, and you have a new look without spending too much money. Often a new floor and a coat of paint are all that's needed, and you don't spend money unnecessarily.

## PAINT

- To prevent skin forming on paint, which can mean having to buy another tin when you need that colour next, replace the lid firmly and hammer it to ensure a tight seal. Then store the tin upside down.
- When about to tackle a major painting job, make sure you measure the room exactly and take those measurements to your paint shop. If you're doing several rooms the same colour, take all the measurements. Even though it's handy to have some extra for touch-ups, two or three litres over could be a little too much and, unless you store it carefully, could be two or three litres paid for and wasted.

## BARGAINS

- Chances are your local newsagent has a bargain renovators' guide to your area. Also look out for a bargain shoppers' guide or a second-hand guide. Many of these are now on the market and can be the first worthwhile investment in your home.
- Check the phone book for companies which specialise in the demolition of old homes and offices, as they may be sources

of the materials you need at a much-reduced rate. Or, alternatively, look for restoration experts or second-hand building suppliers: they usually keep a store of used materials which are in good condition. Depending on what you're after, they won't look much different from something brand-new after a year or so, and if it's an old house you're working on, an old door might be preferable to a new copy.

* The demolition people and second-hand building suppliers are also worth thinking about if you're building or repairing a holiday home — suddenly your little piece of escapism is much more affordable if it's made out of pre-loved materials.

## TOOLS FOR THE JOB

* When thinking about doing the heavy work around the house, consider whether you'll do enough to warrant buying a sander, or ladders, or whatever the job demands. It may be cheaper and easier to rent that piece of equipment and, besides, you won't have to find storage space for it when the job is done. Again, check the phone book (Yellow Pages) and ring around first to compare rates and service. A reputable well-established firm will also have staff on hand who may be able to give you advice on the best way to tackle the project you're thinking about and may be able to suggest a better machine for the job. It never hurts to ask.

* Whether you're buying or hiring, make sure you're familiar with the way the tool operates and the appropriate safety measures. If you're buying, ask the store owner or check with your local building information centre; if you're hiring, check with the company. Either way, there's no money saved if you hurt yourself, or if the job needs to be redone because you haven't learned how to use the machine properly.

* Make sure you have the right safety equipment, for the same reasons. Never tackle any job which means dust and particles will be flying around without goggles, and gloves are always a good idea.

* Don't underestimate the time the job will take, especially if you're hiring equipment. Far better to extend the hiring period than ruin the work trying to get it done in a hurry.

## TEACH YOURSELF

* If you are thinking of building or renovating, look around first for any relevant do-it-yourself courses. It may sound expensive to spend several hundred dollars on a course when you're sure you know what you're doing, but chances are you'll learn a whole lot more, and end up cutting costs and saving much more than you've spent on lessons. It's too easy to dash into the task of renovating and find yourself having to undo some work to do something else because you tackled the tasks in the wrong order.

* Talk to your local building information centre, or a master builders' or architects' association, or check with your local technical college or adult education centre. Even the phone book may list the appropriate avenue to follow.

## INSURANCE

Check on your insurance. Are you, your house and your tradespeople, covered by a household policy should anything go wrong? It's not expensive.

## GLASS BRICKS

One of the most inexpensive ways to bring light into the house, if you don't want the expense of a skylight or new window, is glass bricks. If you don't want to replace a whole wall, why not install a couple of interesting panels? They're an ideal solution in terrace houses or semis which have limited windows. If there is a wall at the end of your terrace with no windows in it, consider knocking out a few bricks and replacing them with glass bricks. They let in some badly needed light and maintain privacy. Glass bricks can span a large area without the need for the expense of reinforcing panels, and they're naturally heat and sound insulated. They're an ideal alternative to solid walls if you're putting a new ensuite in one corner of a master bedroom.

# CENT-SIBLE SHOPPING

- Shop once a fortnight instead of once a week and buy in bigger lots: the less you go into a supermarket, the less often you're tempted. (But remember you have to carry it all.)
- The old rule about never shopping when you're hungry is a good one, particularly with all those easy meals and snacks on the shelves in front of you. The same applies if you're pregnant and going through the craving stage, or if you're having a fit of the PMT or blues cravings.
- Always take a list when you go shopping — and stick to it. And try not to take the children when you're doing the food shopping. They're likely to ask for extras that will cost you money just to keep them quiet.

## SPECIALS

- Check the specials list every week in the paper and buy up when something is reduced in price.
- But don't go out of your way for the specials: it's not much use saving five cents on a tin of dog food when you've travelled halfway across town to pick it up. We're talking specials at your local supermarket or convenience stores.
- These things are often cyclical, so use the specials period to stock up on the necessities at a good price, and regularly.

## PERISHABLES

- Perishables are usually available at cheaper prices just before the close of trade at the end of the day or week. Buy then. The same goes for end of season lines. Food marketers often clear out their old lines, or old packaging, before a new season, so you may find tinned soups a good buy at the end of summer or at the end of winter; cheaper ice cream at the start of autumn; salad dressings at the end of winter or the end of summer. Be sure to check for expiry dates: it's not a bargain if it's out of date by the time you want to use it.
- Here's another idea for perishables. If you can store them or freeze them, buy when you hear there is something that might force a price hike, such as drought or bad weather.

- Always buy fruit and vegetables and meat loose rather than pre-packaged. That way you can be sure of what you're getting.

## HOME BRANDS

It's always worth thinking about home brands. Most of the supermarket's cheaper 'no-name' lines are produced by the companies making the more famous — and costly — name brands.

## BULK BUYING

- Bulk buying is definitely a money-saver, but only when you have the space to store the goods.

- Consider linking up with neighbours or friends to form a cooperative; or if you're buying just for the family, buy only the sort of staples that will keep and that you have storage space for. Tinned tomatoes, tuna and pet food may make sense; bulk flour may not. Buying products in bulk just for the family also may lead to a revolution, when the team decides they're 'sick and tired of...'

## DISPOSABLE ITEMS

Cut back on disposable items on your shopping list. You'll save a lot of money if you use cloth handkerchiefs and serviettes instead of paper ones, and the time and effort spent washing and ironing them is much less of a cost.

## LUNCH

Stop buying lunch every working day. It may only be a few dollars for a sandwich, but chances are you'll grab a drink and maybe some sweets as well. Suddenly you're looking at over $30 every week. Try cutting back and taking lunch from home; you'll save money and it will probably be healthier.

## BARGAIN SHOPPING

• Never overlook markets and street stalls as possible money savers and money earners. Either set up a stall yourself (check with your local council or the market organiser) or check out the bargains. Flea markets, trash and treasure, and car boot sales are all places to hunt a bargain, either new or second-hand.

- Also check the appropriate columns of your local paper: someone may be selling the very something you want. Even major metropolitan papers will list not only markets and stalls and goods on sale privately, but they're a good source of suppliers of second-hand and reconditioned goods. And although auctions can be a trap if you're not careful (for example, spending more than you have on something that's taken your fancy), they can also be great money savers.
- When you are chasing something very specific, don't hesitate to check the Yellow Pages of your phone book. If you find a listing for that particular product, it's easy to ring around and check prices. You then can decide on the supplier you want to use. The Yellow Pages may also give the names of suppliers of samples or seconds of that product, an option you may not have previously considered.
- A good money-saving tip is to look out for the bargain shoppers' guide for your city, or 'Cheap Eats', or a renovators' guide, or any similar compilation. They're usually put together as a result of a lot of legwork by other people and they can save you a great deal of money. Also, they're always looking for suggestions. Maybe you can repay a favour, or give thanks for a good deal someone gave you, by suggesting the publisher lists that supplier in their next issue.
- Save money on books, records and, these days, videos by checking out your nearest second-hand book and video store or book exchange. Not only are you likely to find plenty of bargain reading and viewing, but it's somewhere you can take all your old favourites when you're cleaning out the bookshelves to make way for your new finds.
- If you're taking up a new sport and need the appropriate equipment, consider buying second-hand. It will be cheaper, which might be a worthwhile consideration if the passion turns out to be short-lived. If you're taking golf lessons, ask at the pro shop; the same goes for tennis. They will stock new gear but chances are they have used goods as well, or can point you in the right direction to find some.

# MULTIPURPOSE MONEY SAVERS

There is a whole range of products out there to do a multitude of tasks — and there are quite a few products which will do more than one thing successfully, which is obviously a money saver. We list a few of them.

## BICARBONATE OF SODA

- This is so cheap and so handy you should always have it in the cupboard.
- Keep a packet of bicarbonate of soda in the car. If your baby is sick on the upholstery or on his or her clothes, sprinkle the area with bicarbonate of soda and brush it off when dry. This stops the odour taking hold.
- Wet stains on the carpet or dress fabric? Pour a liberal amount of bicarbonate of soda on the area and vacuum or brush off when dry.
- Mix it with water to make a gentle cleaner for fridge and freezer shelves.
- Rice will be snow-white and fluffy with separate grains if you add a level teaspoon of bicarbonate of soda to the water when it reaches boiling point.
- Ease the pain of sunburn by bathing with bicarbonate of soda in water.
- To remove odour from shoes, sprinkle a thick layer of bicarbonate of soda into the shoes, making sure it goes down to the toe area, then leave for several days. Shake out and air the shoes and you will find all trace of odour gone. Get into the habit of sprinkling bicarbonate of soda in your shoes on a regular basis, particularly in the summer, for odour-free feet.
- Leave a small pack open in the fridge to absorb all the smells.
- Use a cloth and a small amount of bicarbonate of soda to rub into and remove stubborn stains from tea and coffee mugs.
- Use a touch of bicarbonate of soda to ease the pain of mouth ulcers.
- Clean dental plates with a damp toothbrush dipped in it. Add a drop of peppermint oil to deoderise.

- Mix to a paste with water or vinegar to soothe a heat rash or a stinging nettle rash.
- Dissolve several teaspoons in a litre of water and use to remove all build-up from car battery terminals.
- Smelly bottles, particularly children's plastic drink bottles? Put a teaspoon of bicarbonate of soda into the bottle and fill with hot water. Allow to soak for two hours, then rinse well.
- Mix water, white vinegar and bicarbonate of soda for an effective cleaner for almost any cleaning job you can think of.
- Burnt-on food? Fill the affected saucepan or casserole dish with warm water and add 2 tablespoons of bicarbonate of soda. Allow to soak overnight and then wash, rinse and dry as usual.
- To clean dirty combs quickly, put them in hot water and sprinkle with a teaspoon or two of bicarbonate of soda. Leave them for a few minutes, then rinse well.
- You can clean tarnished silver with a paste made of water and bicarbonate of soda. Rub on with a damp sponge and wipe till clean. Then rinse and buff to a shine with a clean, dry cloth.
- Unblock the sink by putting 1 tablespoon of bicarbonate of soda and 3 tablespoons of vinegar into the drain. Allow to fizz before following with a kettleful of boiling water.
- To remove strong food odours such as onion, garlic and fish from wood and plastic surfaces, sprinkle bicarbonate of soda on a damp sponge and rub. Rinse well.
- Clean windows, chrome and laminated plastic with bicarbonate of soda sprinkled on a wet sponge. Polish off with a soft cloth.
- Smelly carpet? Sprinkle well with bicarbonate of soda and leave overnight, then vacuum.
- Clean your oven's glass door with a damp cloth dipped in bicarbonate of soda. Sponge off with a clean damp sponge.
- Stained laminex or enamel stoves can be cleaned by rubbing with a thick paste of bicarbonate of soda and water. Leave for an hour and wipe off.
- Ease the pain of chilblains by applying a paste made of ½ teaspoon of bicarbonate of soda mixed with 1 teaspoon of vinegar.
- Remove perspiration odour from garments made of man-made fibres by dissolving 2 heaped tablespoons of bicarbonate of soda in ¾ bucketful of cold or lukewarm water and soak garments for an hour. Wash as usual after soaking.

# BORAX

- Remember that borax is a poisonous substance, so use and store it carefully.
- Add a dash of borax to some washing-up detergent to wash grime off chrome furniture or fittings.
- To remove yellow spots from stored linen, mix 2 tablespoons of borax in 2 ¼ litres of lukewarm water and soak the fabric overnight. Wash as usual the next day.
- Need to clean painted woodwork? Dissolve 2 tablespoons of borax in boiling water and add to a bowl of lukewarm soapy water. Wash woodwork with a soft cloth wrung out in this mix, rinse and dry thoroughly. If there are fingermarks or greasy stains to lift, add a little paraffin to the soapsuds and follow directions as given.
- Clean a stained bath with borax and lemon juice mixed to a paste; rinse off.

- Remove the dressing from new tea towels by soaking overnight in water with 2 tablespoons of borax added.
- Sprinkle borax into garbage bins to remove the smell.
- When washing tea towels, add a little borax to the water. The towels keep their colour and it removes dirt and grease.

## CLOUDY AMMONIA

- Rub it on aluminium saucepans with a cloth, then polish with a soft cloth to make them shine.
- Clean hairbrushes with warm soapy water and a dash of cloudy ammonia. If the brush has a wooden back, smear it with petroleum jelly before washing. Then rinse and wipe the jelly off and shake the bristles free of water too.
- Old gold jewellery comes up well when dropped into a container of undiluted cloudy ammonia. Leave for around 10 minutes or so, then rinse under cold water and pat dry with a paper towel or a soft cloth. To clean any crevices in the piece, use an old toothbrush dipped in cloudy ammonia.
- Remove cooking grease stains from quarry tiles by rubbing over with a cloth lightly dipped in a teaspoon of cloudy ammonia.
- Make your own silver polishing cloth by cutting a piece of towelling or flannelette (from old sheets or towels) into 30 cm squares and soaking in the following mixture: 1 tablespoon each cloudy ammonia and Goddard's plate powder and 600 mL of water. Soak cloths until all liquid is absorbed and then hang to dry without squeezing out. The cloths are ready to use when dry and should last around six months. This mixture is enough for four 30 cm squares.
- Keep cats away from your favourite plants in the garden by sprinkling cloudy ammonia on a cloth and leaving it near the plant.
- Drinking glasses sometimes go a little cloudy, particularly when they're usually washed in a dishwasher. Try handwashing them in hot soapy water with a dash of cloudy ammonia added.
- Cosmetics around the neckline of a garment can be removed by sponging with a soft cloth dipped in warm water to which a dash of cloudy ammonia has been added.

## CLOVES

- Storing furs? Use a zippered fabric bag. Take an unopened tin of whole cloves and after piercing the sides of the tin to allow the smell of cloves to penetrate the bag, put it inside. Simply replace the tin each year to keep the fur moth-free. (Never store fur in plastic. If you don't have a fabric bag, you can make one out of old sheeting.)
- You can also use tins of cloves with pierced sides in wardrobes and drawers as a more odorously appealing anti-moth weapon.
- Add a few drops of oil of cloves or oil of rose or lavender to your furniture cream or polish to give a subtle perfume to the house.
- Make a cup of tea with a refreshing difference and add 3 cloves to the leaves in the pot.

## EPSOM SALTS

• Toss a light sprinkling of Epsom salts around the roots of ferns after watering them. It makes them, especially maidenhair, grow beautifully.

• Baby clothes gone yellow? Soak them in water to which one packet of Epsom salts has been added.

• To take the stiff dressing out of fabrics before sewing, soak them overnight in a tub of cold water with 60 g Epsom salts added. Rinse well the next day, then wash as usual before using.

• Want to keep your feet cool and dry in the summer? Dissolve some Epsom salts in methylated spirits. Pat the lotion onto your feet and allow to dry before dusting with talcum powder.

• Keep flowers from falling off their vines by watering well around the roots and then sprinkling the ground with 500 g of Epsom salts. Then water well again.

• Washing colourful florals for the first time? Dissolve a packet of Epsom salts in cold water and rinse the fabric in the solution, then wash the usual way. The colours will not run.

- Using Epsom salts is another method for storing furs. Sprinkle the furs with Epsom salts, wrap in tissue paper and put in a fabric (not plastic) bag with some more salts. When needed, just shake out the salts and go — there's no nasty smell to worry about.
- Clean a straw hat by rubbing it over with a mix of ¼ teaspoon Epsom salts, the juice of 1 lemon, 1 teaspoon of salt and a little lukewarm water.
- Store suede, leather and plastic shoes in plastic bags with Epsom salts. Seal the bags. Just shake out the salts when the shoes are needed.
- New towels? Soak them in cold water with a handful of Epsom salts. This removes the dressing and makes them soft and absorbent. Wash as usual before using.
- Clean coloured tile grouting with a little Epsom salts on a soft wet brush (an old toothbrush or nailbrush would be ideal): white grouting needs a dash of bleach in the scrubbing water.

## LEMONS

- To remove nicotine stains from your fingers, take the juice of 1 lemon and mix it with equal parts of olive oil and 1 tablespoon of salt. Shake well and rub into your fingers twice a day.
- If your patent leather shoes have dried out, rub them with lemon juice and allow it to dry before polishing in the usual way. Lemon juice will also clean black and tan shoes: rub briskly and polish well.
- Warts can often be cured by applying a mixture of equal parts lemon juice, castor oil and kerosene three times a day for a week.
- Adding a few slices of lemon to the water when cooking cabbage improves the flavour and reduces the odour.
- Remove perspiration marks from woollen garments by sponging with lemon juice and water. Hang to air.
- Drizzle grilling steaks or chops with a little lemon juice and some butter for a delightful flavour and more tender meat.
- Mix equal parts of glycerine and lemon juice and keep near the sink. Rub it into your hands while they are still wet.
- Washing up after a meal of fish? Toss the used lemons into the washing-up water to kill the fishy smell.
- Clean a stained kettle by putting lemon skins inside the vessel and boiling with water. Then allow to stand overnight and rinse clean in the morning.
- Clean tarnished brass and copper with pure lemon juice. Simply wipe over the surface with a cloth liberally wet with juice (or perhaps soak smaller objects in a glass dish with juice); leave for a minute or two, then dry and rub with a soft cloth.
- A slice of lemon dipped in salt will remove stains on terrazzo floors. Rub the stain well and then leave for an hour before washing as usual.
- The cigarette smoker has gone but the smell remains? Leave a bucket or bowl of water in the room with several slices of lemon in it to absorb the smell.
- Use half a lemon to brighten dulled leather on chairs. Simply rub the chair with it and then polish with a soft cloth.
- If your iron has some brown stains on it, rub with a cut lemon when cold and then wipe over with a damp cloth and polish with a dry one.
- Washing glassware? Put a few lemon skins in the rinsing water to add shine.

- Remove wood stains or onion, garlic or fish odours from your hands by rubbing with a slice of lemon or some lemon juice.
- Try shifting a headache by drinking a mix of the juice of 1 lemon and ½ teaspoon of bicarbonate of soda. Drink while it's fizzing.
- Clean stainless steel by rubbing with lemon peel and then washing with pure hot soapy water.

## METHYLATED SPIRITS

- If you're planning do a lot of walking, you can prevent blisters by rubbing your feet with methylated spirits daily for a week before the big march.
- Put 1 or 2 drops of methylated spirits on a piece of cottonwool and use to rub away heat marks on furniture. Polish in the usual way.
- Gilt photo or picture frames looking a little discoloured? Wipe over with a mix of equal parts methylated spirits and water, then dry well and buff with a soft cloth.
- Clean glass in picture frames with methylated spirits — water may seep through frames and damage the picture. Wipe on with a piece of tissue or cloth and wipe off with another.
- Another way to clean old gold jewellery is by soaking in a small china cup filled with methylated spirits. Swirl the jewellery around gently and brush with an old soft toothbrush. Lift out of the cup and allow to air-dry before rubbing with a soft cloth.
- Keep laminated surfaces shining by rubbing over with methylated spirits on a soft cloth.
- Prevent bathroom mirrors from fogging up by wiping over with a cloth dipped in equal quantities of glycerine and methylated spirits. Then polish with a soft cloth.
- Moss on the brick path? Remove it by painting methylated spirits over it.
- If you want to stop newly painted white woodwork from going yellow, particularly if it's in the kitchen, take a piece of cotton knit fabric (an old singlet or T-shirt) and wring it out in warm soapy water. Now sprinkle it with a solution of equal parts of methylated spirits and kerosene. Wipe the woodwork once a week.
- Another way to make your own silver polishing cloth is by mixing 1 tablespoon of methylated spirits with 1 teaspoon of silver cleaning powder and 1 cup of cold water. Cut a piece of flannelette or towelling into a 46 cm square and soak this in the mixture till the liquid is totally absorbed. Hang out to dry without squeezing. Store in a plastic bag and use to rub up a shine on any silver. It will last for several years.
- Silverware will shine if polished with a paste of starch and methylated spirits: moisten about 1 tablespoon of starch with the spirits. Rub onto silver and allow to dry, then rub off. Store silver in aluminium foil to prevent tarnishing.
- Sprinkle a little methylated spirits on your clothes brush before brushing dark clothing to help lift those annoying little specks.

## PETROLEUM JELLY (VASELINE)

- Its most obvious use is probably on baby's bottom to help prevent nappy rash, or to heal and prevent cradle cap on baby's head.

* Taking off an adhesive strip? Massage the edges with jelly so it pulls off without a major 'ouch'.

* Use it on lips or noses to prevent and heal chapping.

* Put a thin layer into the candlestick holder to make wax removal easy.

* Put it on patent leather shoes and handbags to make them shine and prevent cracking. Rub a little bit well into the leather.

* Stroke some onto eyelashes to make them shine and look longer, or on eyebrows to smooth them in the direction you want. It will also soothe the delicate skin under the eyebrow after plucking.

* Rub it on the tracks of your bedroom and kitchen drawers to make them slide more easily.

* Your favourite lipstick almost finished? Scrape out the leftovers and mix with equal amounts of petroleum jelly to make a super coloured lip gloss. Or use it on its own as a plain lip gloss.

* Smear it on nuts and bolts which won't move easily to help work them loose.

* When giving yourself a manicure or pedicure at home, smooth petroleum jelly over the whole hand or foot and massage well. It smooths skin, softens cuticles and makes your hands and feet feel better.

* When you're doing some painting around the house, rub some well into your hands to make paint splashes easier to remove; and rub it on the fixtures in the areas where you're painting to make cleaning up easier. Use a paintbrush or small scraper to put a layer onto window glass before painting the frame.

* Dyeing your hair at home? Smooth a thin layer on the skin around the hairline to prevent the dye staining your skin.

* Apply a touch of jelly to hinges of windows, doors and cupboards to stop squeaks, and apply to the axles of rollerblades to speed them up.

* Protect anything that's prone to rust by regularly smearing the metal fixtures and fittings with a little petroleum jelly.

* Stop your swimming goggles or mask from leaking by rubbing jelly around the inside edge.

* Prevent chafing to hands, feet and thighs in sporting activities, by smearing jelly on the area likely to be affected. This includes covering the whole foot with a thin layer of jelly before putting on shoes and socks.

* Smear a little jelly on your forehead before a game of tennis, or any energetic activity. It stops perspiration running into your eyes.

* To stop mud clinging to sports shoes with spikes, put some jelly on the soles.

* Rust marks on the iron can be removed by rubbing with petroleum jelly. Leave for two days, then clean off with ammonia.

* Smear the corroded area of your kettle with petroleum jelly and leave for an hour or two before adding 1 cup of bicarbonate of soda and filling the kettle with clear water. Bring to the boil and allow to boil slowly for several minutes. Then let stand overnight. Any corrosion that remains the next day can be scrubbed off with a metal pot scourer. Rinse several times with very hot water before using again.

# SALT

* Make a paste of salt, bicarbonate of soda and lemon juice to clean stained white

polythene cutting boards.

• Sprinkle salt on red wine stains and vacuum up when dry.

• Eliminate water and mildew stains from blinds by dampening the blind and rubbing with ordinary soap that has been rubbed in salt. Put the damp blind out in the sun to dry. Then cover the blind with a paste made of fuller's earth, water and ordinary soap; leave for 12 hours before washing off.

• Clean the dust off artificial flowers by putting them in a large paper bag containing a cup or two of salt and shaking well.

• Remove tea and coffee stains from tablecloths by rubbing salt into the cloth after rinsing with cold water. This usually only works with fresh stains.

• Remove stains from a teak table by mixing salt and olive oil to a liquidy paste and rubbing on the stains. Leave for a short time before buffing off with a soft cloth.

## TEA TREE OIL

• It comes as a pure oil, diluted oil, body lotion or soap and skin wash. Check directions on the label for other uses.

• Wash cuts and abrasions thoroughly and then apply oil two or three times a day with a cottonwool ball to stop infection.

• Dab on mosquito stings and insect bites to ease the itch.

• For muscular aches and pains, massage well before and after exercise with a few drops of oil blended with avocado or sweet almond oil, or add a teaspoon to a hot bath and soak.

• Rub tea tree lotion into dry skin, cracked heels, sunburn and skin irritations including chafing, nappy rash and shaving rash.

• For minor burns, flush the burn with cold water and then apply pure oil directly to the damaged skin.

• For nasal, bronchial and sinus congestion, dilute 1 teaspoon in hot water for an inhalation.

• Apply to a cold sore or pimple as soon as it appears and use three or four times a day until the sore or pimple is gone.

• For a sore throat, add 4 drops to 25 mL of warm water and gargle two or three times a day. BEWARE: Do not swallow!

• Washing the dog? Add 5 to 10 drops of oil to the shampoo and leave on for a few minutes before rinsing.

## VINEGAR

Always keep plenty of white vinegar on hand as it is cheap and has lots of uses.

• Clean stained kettles, coffeepots and teapots by filling with hot water and adding half a cup of vinegar. Allow to stand for several hours, then brush and rinse out.

• Clean inside a steam iron by filling it with a mixture of 2 dessertspoons each of white vinegar and distilled water. Put the hot iron on a cake cooler covered with an old towel and allow to drain through.

• Remove cat or dog hair from the carpet or upholstery by squeezing out a sponge in equal parts vinegar and water and wiping the hairs off the surface.

• Remove stains from leather by wiping over them with a cloth dampened with warm water and vinegar. Restore the polish by rubbing hard with a cloth dipped in raw linseed oil.

• Another treatment for cloudy drinking glasses is to put a little salt and vinegar on the dishwashing sponge and wash them with this. Then rinse well in hot water.

• New flannelette sheets? Before using, soak them overnight in water to cover, with a handful of salt and a tablespoon of vinegar added. Rinse them the next day with clean water to which you have added half a cup of Epsom salts and hang them out to dry. This will prevent pilling.

• Hard paintbrushes will soften after an hour or so if left standing in a jar of hot vinegar.

• To cure hiccoughs, take 1 teaspoon of brown sugar moistened with a little white vinegar.

• Take the sting out of insect bites and mosquito bites by dabbing the affected area with vinegar and bicarbonate of soda.

• Pep up tired French-polished furniture by using this mixture. Combine ½ cup raw linseed oil, ¼ cup turpentine, 1 cup methylated spirits and 1 ½ cups vinegar. Shake well and wash the surface, wiping this on with a cloth. Allow to stand for a minute or two, wipe dry and then polish with another clean cloth.

• Another good furniture polish can be made by mixing 1 cup each of vinegar and paraffin with ½ cup of linseed oil. Add a few drops of oil of cloves or oil of lavender; bottle and shake well before using. Apply with a soft cloth. This mix is good for all painted furniture.

• Scratches on the furniture? Mix one part vinegar to two parts olive oil and rub on with a soft cloth. This is particularly good for dark furniture.

• Mildew on the furniture? Put 1 tablespoon of vinegar into half a litre of warm water and rub this over the mildew with a soft cloth. Then wipe off with another soft cloth, dry and polish as usual.

• Wiping the inside of your fridge with vinegar will help prevent mould.

• Vinegar and cooking salt are a good combination to lift stains from baths, basins and sinks.

• Rust marks on baths or enamel sinks will come clean if rubbed with a cloth dipped in vinegar.

• Boil some vinegar in a new frying pan before you use it and food won't stick.

• Put 1 to 2 cups of vinegar in a bucket of warm water for washing glass, chrome, tiles and enamel surfaces.

• Help yourself to relief from corns and bunions by rubbing them with a little vinegar every night.

• Save money by not buying hook-on toilet cleaners: they have very little value in terms of cleaning and disinfecting, and they pollute the environment. You can use vinegar neat with plenty of elbow grease to clean the toilet.

• Clean mould off the tiles and grouting with vinegar.

• For mould on leather book covers, wipe over with a soft cloth wrung out in vinegar.

• Rusty cake tins? Fill them with warm water and a teaspoon of vinegar and allow to stand overnight. Wash off rust in the morning.

• Remove dirty marks from porous brick fireplaces by dabbing with a rag dipped in vinegar. This also brings out the natural colour of the bricks.

• A good floor polish is made by mixing together 250 mL each of kerosene and vinegar. Shake well and apply with a

sponge mop. It's also good for cleaning furniture, marble, paintwork and tiles.
* To clean discoloured decanters and small-necked bottles, mix a tablespoon each of vinegar and fresh tea leaves with some water. Pour this into the bottle and shake well. Then rinse.
* See also the chapter Food and Cooking.

# DOING THE LAUNDRY

## WASHING WITH …

• See the chapter Multipurpose Money Savers for other tips about washing, using ordinary household products.

• Vinegar can be used as a disinfectant. Add a cup to the bucket in which baby's cloth nappies are soaking.

• Do you need to bleach the nappies during the wash? Lemon juice is the answer, also around one cupful.

• Add a handful of bicarbonate of soda to the final rinse when washing nappies to remove all traces of soap and ammonia and to help prevent nappy rash.

• Add ¼ cup of vinegar to the final rinse on washday. This is as good a fabric softener as the most expensive commercial preparations.

• Add 1 cup of vinegar to the final rinse when washing sheets. This will keep the fluff and lint away from them.

• Remove make-up marks from the neckline of a garment by rubbing with stale bread. The bread needs to be at least two days old.

• To wash and soften woollens, dissolve 60 g of borax in 1 L of hot water. Then pour the solution into 4 L of lukewarm water and add 1 teaspoon of vinegar. Soak woollens in the mix for 5 minutes, then squeeze out gently and hang to dry.

• Or make your own woollen soap mix. Combine 4 cups of Lux Flakes, 1 cup of methylated spirits and 50 mL of double-distilled eucalyptus oil in a jar. The flakes do not dissolve. To wash the woollens, add 2 tablespoons to half a bucket of hot water. It's not necessary to rinse it out afterwards but it won't matter if you do. For really dirty woollens, allow to soak for 5 or 10 minutes. Press and knead until very clean, then squeeze thoroughly and hang to dry. If the water is really dirty, add another 2 ¼ litres of clean water to the suds and wash again; then squeeze and hang to dry. This recipe is also good for washing dogs, but they must be rinsed afterwards!

• Think about changing from commercial washing powders which are expensive and quite damaging to the environment. Instead, use one part washing soda (sodium carbonate, not sodium Bicarbonate) mixed with three parts pure soap flakes. But before you convert to pure soap, wash your clothes in washing soda first to remove the detergent residue and avoid yellowing. From then on, always treat stains before washing.

## WASHING MACHINES

* Small loads of washing cost you more in terms of power, water and soap powder. Wait till you have enough dirty clothes for a full-size load. A conventional automatic washing machine will use around 200 litres of water to complete the wash cycle. But don't overload the machine; it won't operate as efficiently and may cause a breakdown.
* Wash like items together so clothes are washed evenly.
* Handwash small items in a sink or basin rather than making them a small load in the machine, and hang them out to dry rather than using the drier.
* Read the amount of detergent that's required and then cut it back by at least one-third. It's in the soap manufacturer's interest for you to use the product quickly. That particular amount isn't necessarily a magic formula for cleaner clothes.
* A washing machine with a 'suds saving' device is a real money saver and worth the investment. One lot of detergent will handle two or three loads, or you can add a little boost of powder between each load. At the end of the wash, siphon off the water to water lawns and shrubs, particularly if you're using an ecologically friendly detergent.
* Connect your washing machine to cold water. You may need to dissolve your powder first but you save in terms of water and energy.
* Ready to buy a new washing machine but puzzled what to buy? A front-loading machine will use less energy and less water than a top-loader and is gentler on clothes. A top-loader, however, often comes with variable water levels so that you can make the adjustment to suit the size of the load. That said, it is always more economical to wash one full load rather than several smaller ones.
* To keep your machine clear of lint and soap build-up, put 2 tablespoons of Epsom salts into warm water in the machine and run through a full cycle. If you don't have Epsom salts, use 2 cups of vinegar. Do this once every month or two to keep the machine clean.
* If the water in your area is particularly hard, talk to your plumber about the cost of installing a special water-softening system. This could save you a fortune in the cost of your detergents and cleaning powders.

## CLOTHES DRIERS

* Make your clothes drier work better for you by cleaning the lint filter after each load or before putting one in. Make it a habit.
* Make sure the outside vent is also unclogged. And, remember, there are very few things that need a 'hot' cycle which uses a huge amount of power. Switch to 'warm' or 'cool'. Yes, it takes a little longer but it still uses less power than a 'hot' run.
* Make sure your drier is set up in a dry, warm and well-ventilated area. Humid, cold air increases the amount of power you need. If it's possible, connect your drier to an external outlet so the moist air is not constantly being used because of the strain it puts on the machine (read, more power, more money). Alternatively, open doors

and windows if it's a dry day when the machine is operating.

• Just as with a stove, don't open the door of the drier too often during a cycle. Lost heat means more power is needed.

• Don't place soaking wet clothes into the drier; it puts too great a load on the mechanism, which equals extra energy. Don't overload, and don't overdry. They're all energy-expending habits.

• Save on ironing time by hanging clothes as soon as you take them out of the drier. The heat will help to smooth wrinkles; gravity also will do much of the work.

# IRONING

## IRON MAINTENANCE

Steam irons are another item which need simple but regular maintenance. Make sure you unclog the vents of the chemical build-up that occurs. If the iron isn't working properly, it will take longer to do the ironing and use more power. You can buy special iron cleaners at most supermarkets or hardware stores. Or consider using demineralised water; you can buy it in large bottles from the supermarket. Or invest in one of the small shaker demineraliser bottles and make up the demineralised water as you need it.

## IRONING TIPS

• It sounds like hard and dull work, but try to iron a full load of washing in one hit. You save power and money by not turning the iron on and off and waiting for it to heat up again.

• When you're nearing the end of the load of ironing that you're doing, turn the iron off. The residual heat will take care of that last hanky or table serviette.

## IRONING AIDS

• Save on the cost of commercially prepared ironing aids: simply sprinkle linen tablecloths, napkins and clothes that are difficult to iron with water. Place them in a garbage bag and cook in the microwave on high for around 1 or 2 minutes, or until warm. Then the stubborn creases will iron out with ease.

• Make your own spray starch: mix 1 heaped dessertspoon of cornflour in 200 mL of cold water, making sure there are no lumps. Stir into 300 mL of boiling water and keep stirring until water boils again and the mixture thickens. Then pour the mixture into 500 mL cold water, using more or less for desired thickness. Pour into spray bottles and use on clothes that require a little extra stiffening. Add some drops of perfume if desired.

# INDEX

Borrowing and budgeting 69–72
  Buying a home 70
  Setting a budget 71

Cars 25–29
  Buying 25
  Getting around 26
  Running costs 27
  Safety 28
Cleaning up the savings 9
Entertainment and travel 11–16
  Entertainment 13
    Film and theatre 13
    Fitness 13
    Libraries 13
    Museums 13
    Parties 13
  Travel 15
  Wining and dining 13
    Babysitting 11
    Dining in 11
    Dining out 12
    The great outdoors 12

Fashion 31–33
  Chic bargains 31
  Clothing care 33
  Kids' clothing 33
  New uses for clothes 32
  Recycling fashion 31
Food and cooking 35–43
  A seven-day menu 38
  Dairy products 36
  Eggs 38
  Fruit and vegetables 37
  Leftovers 38
  Making your own 42
    Dog biscuits 42
    Fromage frais 42
    Soft cheese 42
    Sundried tomatoes 43
    Tia Maria 43
    Yeast 43
    Yogurt 43
  Meat, fish and poultry 35

  Plan ahead 40
  Special treats 39
  Party food 40
    Potato nests 42

Gardening 45–52
  Bananas 46
  Companion planting 47
  Composting 48
  Fruit and vegetables 46
  Green thinking 45
  Indoor plants 46
  Planting to save energy 18
  Propagation 45
  Sprays 50
  Tea leaves 50
  Watering 51
Gifts 57–59
  Cards and giftwrap 57
  Gifts 57

Health, hygiene and beauty 61–68
  For freshening the air 66
  For your face and hands and skin 66
  For your health 68
    Making cough drops 68
    Making cough mixture 68
    Making liniment 68
    Making vapour rub 68
  Hair care 63
    Herbal shampoo 64
    Shampoo 64
  Healthy beauty 62
  Saving with soap 64
  Soap making 64
    Basic soft soap 65
    Creamy white soap 65
    For all cleansing 64
    Herbal and scented soap 65
Heating, cooling and lighting 17–23

  Airconditioning 19
  Bedding 19
  Building 17
  Electrical appliances 19
  Plants 18
  Heating 20
    Electric or gas 21
    Hot water 22
    Keeping the heat 21
    Lighting 22
    Pot belly stoves 20
    Solar power 23
    Wood fires 20

Ironing 111
  Iron maintenance 111
  Ironing aids 111
  Ironing tips 111

Laundry 109–111
  Clothes driers 110
  Washing 109
  Washing machines 110
Money savers 99–108
  Bicarbonate of soda 99
  Borax 100
  Cloudy ammonia 101
  Cloves 101
  Epsom salts 102
  Lemons 103
  Methylated spirits 104
  Petroleum jelly (vaseline) 104
  Salt 105
  Tea tree oil 106
  Vinegar 106
Money-saving tips 53–56
  Dishwashers 55
  Home and health hints 53
  Shopping 54
  Telephone calls 55
  Whitegoods 56
Office savings 73–75
  Around the office 74
  Equipment 75
  Paper 73
  Refurnishing 75

Pest control 77–83
  Ants 77
  Aphids 77
  Blowflies 78
  Borers 78
  Cockroaches 78
  Crickets 79
  Earwigs 79
  Fleas 79
  Flies 79
  Fruit fly 80
  Lice 81
  Mice 81
  Mites 81
  Mosquitos 81
  Moths 82
  Possums 82
  Sandflies 82
  Silverfish 82
  Slugs 83
  Snails 83
    Snail spray 1 83
    Snail spray 2 83
  Termites 83
  Weevils 83

Recycling 85–88
Renovating 89–93
  Bargains 91
  Bathrooms 89
  Glass bricks 93
  Insurance 92
  Kitchens 90
  Paint 91
  Teach yourself 92
  Tools for the job 92
  Walls and floors 89

Shopping 95–98
  Bargain shopping 97
  Bulk buying 96
  Disposable items 96
  Home brands 96
  Lunch 97
  Perishables 95
  Specials 95